MW00629526

The Paraclete

A Manual of Instruction and Devotion

by

FATHER MARIANUS FIEGE, O.M.CAP.

TAN Books
Charlotte, North Carolina

| Nihil obstat: | H. Alerding |
| | Censor Deputatus |

Imprimatur:	☩ Michael Augustine
	Archbishop of New York
	August 15, 1899

Nihil obstat:	Fr. Joannes Maria A Lynn Regis. O.M.Cap.
	Fr. Laurentius A Bristol, O.M.Cap
	Censores Deputati
	June 21, 1890

Imprimatur:	Fr. Bernardus A Cestria, O.M.Cap.
	Min. Prov. Angliae
	July 20, 1899

Retypeset in 2012 by TAN Books.

ISBN: 978-0-89555-131-3

Printed and bound in India.

TAN Books
Charlotte, North Carolina
www.TANBooks.com
2012

Dedication

These pages written in honor of God, the Holy Ghost are most humbly and most lovingly inscribed to Mary Immaculate Spouse of the Holy Ghost to the end that all who devoutly use this little volume may walk more worthily of their vocation as becometh the sons of God, the Father through the merits of Jesus Christ His Son in the Power of the Holy Ghost and By Mary's own most singular intercession

Pope Leo XIII on Devotion to the Holy Ghost

"We earnestly desire that . . . piety may increase and be inflamed towards the Holy Ghost, to Whom especially all of us owe the graces of following the paths of truth and virtue.

"All preachers and those having care of souls should remember that it is their duty to instruct their people more diligently and more fully about the Holy Ghost. . . . What should be chiefly dwelt upon and clearly explained is the multitude and greatness of the benefits which have been bestowed, and are constantly bestowed upon us, by this Divine Giver.

"We decree and command that throughout the Catholic Church this year, and every subsequent year, a Novena shall take place before Whit-Sunday in all parish churches."

(Encyclical, May 9, 1897.)

Contents

Preface xvii

Part First

  I. God the Father 1
      1. God the Father made you 1
      2. God made you for Himself 1
      3. God made you to be His child 2
      4. God adopts you through His Son
         made Man. 2
  II. God the Son 2
      1. God the Son redeemed you 2
      2. Jesus Christ—the Way, the Truth, and
         the Life 3
      3. Jesus Christ entrusted the means of
         salvation to His Church. 4
      4. The means of salvation are applied to you
         by the Holy Ghost. 4
 III. God the Holy Ghost 5
      1. God the Holy Ghost sanctifies you 5
      2. The Holy Ghost abides within you. 5

3. The Holy Ghost is the Bond of Union
   between you and God 6
4. The Holy Ghost casts off no one 6
5. The Holy Ghost is the Fount of Light and
   Strength 7
6. The Holy Ghost is your Comforter 8
7. God is to be glorified for all He has done
   for you 9
8. The Holy Ghost to be glorified in an
   especial manner. 10

IV. The Holy Ghost and Jesus Christ 10
1. Jesus Christ given by the Holy Ghost. . . .10
2. The World prepared for the coming of the
   Redeemer by the Holy Ghost 10
3. The Mother of the Redeemer prepared by
   the Holy Ghost. 11
4. The Mystery of the Incarnation accom-
   plished by the Holy Ghost. 11
5. The Sacred Manhood of Jesus endowed
   with the gifts of the Holy Ghost 12
6. The Divinity of Jesus Christ manifested by
   the Holy Ghost. 12
7. Jesus Christ guided in all His actions by
   the Holy Ghost. 13
8. Jesus Christ still on earth through the
   operation of the Holy Ghost 14

V. The Holy Ghost and the Church. 14

1. The Mission of Jesus Christ perpetuated by His Church. 14

2. The Church owes her existence to the Holy Ghost .15

3. The Church extended and preserved by the Holy Ghost 15

4. The Church sanctified and glorified by the Holy Ghost 16

VI. The Holy Ghost and the Means of Salvation .17

1. To the Holy Ghost you owe the gift of Divine Adoption 17

2. The Holy Ghost makes you like unto Jesus the Son of God 18

3. The Holy Ghost your stay and support . .18

4. To the Holy Ghost you owe the gift of prayer 18

5. The Holy Ghost imparts strength to do penance. 19

6. Without the aid of the Holy Ghost you cannot do good nor avoid evil 19

7. The outward means of Salvation, administered by the Church made efficacious by the Holy Ghost 19

8. The Holy Ghost enables you to respect and obey law and authority 20

9. Extraordinary means of Salvation made efficacious by the Holy Ghost 20

VII. The Church, the Ordinary Channel by which
     the Holy Ghost dispenses His Graces and
     Gifts 21
     1. The Work of the Holy Ghost universal. . .21
     2. The Work of the Holy Ghost different as
        to times and circumstances 22
     3. The Action of the Holy Ghost not confined
        to the Visible Church 23
     4. The Operations of the Holy Ghost not
        absolutely dependent on the Sacraments .24
     5. Obedience to the Church a sure test of
        being led by the Spirit of God 25
VIII. Special Devotion to the Holy Ghost 26
     1. What it means 26
     2. What special devotion to the Holy Ghost
        will do. 27
     3. Special marks of the true servant of the
        Holy Ghost 30
     4. Exhortation to practice special devotion to
        the Holy Ghost .31
IX. The Holy Ghost and the Priesthood 33
     1. Call to the Sacred Priesthood a special
        grace of the Holy Ghost 33
     2. The dignity of the Priesthood closely
        resembles that of the Divine Maternity . .33
     3. The office of the Priesthood a communica-
        tion of the office of the Holy Ghost. 34

4. The Priest another Christ by the power of the Holy Ghost .35

5. Devotion to the Holy Ghost a great help to the Priest and his people 36

X. The Holy Ghost and Religious Orders. 37

1. Call to the Religious State a special grace of the Holy Ghost 37

2. Religious Orders the special work of the Holy Ghost 38

3. Exhortation to Religious to practice devotion to the Holy Ghost. 39

XI. The Holy Ghost and Devotion to the Sacred Heart of Jesus 40

1. Devotion to the Holy Ghost promotes devotion to the Sacred Heart. 40

2. Devotion to the Holy Ghost makes you truly one with the Sacred Heart. 40

3. Exhortation to lovers of the Sacred Heart. 41

XII. The Holy Ghost and Devotion to the Blessed Virgin Mary 41

XIII. The Holy Ghost and the Souls in Purgatory .42

XIV. The Holy Ghost and the Works of Mercy . . .43

XV. The Holy Ghost and those engaged in Study or Teaching. 44

XVI. The Holy Ghost and those zealous for the spread of Faith 45

XVII. Devotion to the Holy Ghost especially
       commended to the Young. 46
XVIII. Devotion to the Holy Ghost an especial
       antidote against the evils of the day 47

Part Second

  I. Daily Acts 51
      1. Morning Prayers 51
      2. During the Day 53
      3. Night Prayers. 57
 II. The Holy Sacrifice of the Mass 59
      1. Mass the Sacrifice of the New Law. 59
      2. The four great ends of Mass 60
      3. A devout method of hearing Mass 61
III. Confession 69
      1. The Power of the Sacrament of Penance . .69
      2. Method of Confession 70
 IV. Holy Communion 79
      1. The last will of Jesus. 79
      2. Preparation for Holy Communion. 80
      3. Thanksgiving after Holy Communion . . .88
      4. Indulgenced Prayer after Communion . . .93
      5. Divine Praises .94
      6. Soul of Christ .95

Part Third

Special Exercises in honor of God the Holy Ghost

I. Daily Act of Consecration to the Holy
Ghost 97

II. Prayer of St. Francis of Assisi for the gift of
the Divine Spirit 98

III. Divine Praises in honor of God the Holy
Ghost 98

IV. Prayer of the Servants of the Holy Ghost. . . .99

V. Prayer of a soul in deep distress 100

VI. Canticle to the Holy Ghost 101

VII. Seven invocations to the Holy Ghost. 103

VIII. Litany of the Holy Ghost 105

IX. Little Office of the Holy Ghost 109

X. Chaplet of the Holy Ghost 116

1. Notice on the Chaplet of the Holy
Ghost 116

2. Method of reciting the Chaplet 117

3. Method of public recital of the Chaplet. .123

4. Brief Reflections on the five Mysteries
of the Chaplet .133

5. Acts of Praise and Thanksgiving. 135

XI. Devout Exercises in honor of God the Holy
Ghost for each day in the week. 137

1. Sunday—Adoration. 137

2. Monday—Esteem 139

3. Tuesday—Joy 140
4. Wednesday—Grief 142
5. Thursday—Thanksgiving 143
6. Friday—Condolence 145
7. Saturday—Petition 147
XII. The Divine Office for Pentecost Sunday . . .149
1. Notice 149
2. Prayer before Divine Office 151
3. Matins and Lauds 151
4. Prayer after Divine Office 183
5. Prime 184
6. Terce 192
7. Sext 200
8. None 206
9. Vespers 213
10. Compline 224
XIII. Mass of the Holy Ghost for Pentecost
Sunday 233
XIV. The Sacrament of Confirmation 238
1. Confirmation the completion of the
Sacrament of Baptism 238
2. Preparation for the Sacrament of
Confirmation 240
3. A Prayer for the Seven Gifts of the Holy
Ghost 243
4. Rite of Confirmation 244
5. Thanksgiving after Confirmation 249

     6. Prayer on the anniversary of
       Confirmation .253

XV. Devout Exercise of Reparation for the Sins
    committed against the Holy Ghost. 254
     1. Notice 254
     2. Preparatory Prayer 254
     3. First Reflection—The sin of Presuming
       on God's Mercy. 255
     4. Prayer of Reparation 257
     5. Second Reflection—The sin of Despair .258
     6. Third Reflection—The sin of Resisting
       the Known Truth. 259
     7. Fourth Reflection—The sin of Envying
       another's spiritual good 261
     8. Fifth Reflection—The sin of Obstinacy
       in sin. 263
     9. Sixth Reflection—The sin of Final
       Impenitence .265

XVI. Novena in honor of God the Holy Ghost . .267
     1. The first Novena 267
     2. How to make the Novena 269
     3. Particular directions. 270
     4. Pope Leo XIII on the Novena of
       Pentecost. 271
     5. Reflection for each day of the Novena . .272
     6. The Sequence *Veni, Sancte Spiritus* 273
     7. First Day of the Novena. 274

    8. Second Day of the Novena 279

    9. Third Day of the Novena 283

   10. Fourth Day of the Novena 286

   11. Fifth Day of the Novena 290

   12. Sixth Day of the Novena 294

   13. Seventh Day of the Novena 298

   14. Eighth Day of the Novena 302

   15. Ninth Day of the Novena 306

XVII. The Seven Gifts and the Twelve Fruits of the

       Holy Ghost 312

    1. Notice 312

    2. Wisdom—Charity 314

    3. Understanding—Peace 314

    4. Knowledge—Joy 315

    5. Counsel—Benignity—Goodness 315

    6. Fortitude—Patience—Longanimity 316

    7. Piety—Faith—Mildness 317

    8. Fear of the Lord—Modesty—Continency

       —Chastity 317

XVIII. Seven Special Promises from Holy Writ . . .318

    1. Notice 318

    2. Divine Adoption 318

    3. Divine Endowment 318

    4. Participation in the Spirit of Jesus

       Christ 319

    5. Gift of Prayer 319

    6. Strength to do God's Holy Will 319

    7. The Fruit of the Spirit 319
    8. Life Everlasting 320
XIX. Practices Suggested 320
XX. Pious Union in Honor of God the Holy
      Ghost. 323

The Paraclete

MANUAL OF INSTRUCTION AND DEVOTION

Preface

The human soul is a spirit created to animate a material body, within which it is confined, and through which it is tied down, at present, to this visible world. Yet, at the same time, it gives evidence of a strong and irrepressible tendency to break through its barriers, raise itself above this physical universe, and hold converse with the inhabitants of the unseen world. Whence arises this tendency? It may, to some extent, be quite natural; for the soul, being spiritual, would naturally tend to commune with beings of its own kind. Yet the real cause must be attributed to the fact that God destined man for supernatural union with Himself, which implies the raising of man to a state beyond his natural condition; and hence there springs up within the soul a natural and indestructible longing for something beyond the whole world, implanted in his heart by God Himself. As long as man aspires to this supernatural union, all is well with him. He will find therein true peace and contentment, which is a foretaste of that unspeakable joy and happiness with which his whole being will be replenished when that union is perfected in heaven.

Yet, at all times, men have been found who, through either blindness or perversity, have deliberately turned aside from God and placed their final end in some other object. But the soul's true nature and instinct ever assert themselves, in spite of man's endeavors to the contrary; and from the lowest depth of the human soul there is heard a strong cry for something beyond this world even then when God is lost sight of and rejected. And what is the result? Attempts are made to place oneself in communication with the spirits of the other world. In many instances, it ends in mere sham and trickery, practiced upon a credulous crowd by impostors. Yet, it also happens that, by a just permission of God, such rash attempts are actually realized and finally result, directly or indirectly, in positive demon-worship, by whatever innocent or high-sounding name it may disguise its real nature. And although practices of this kind have existed at all times, it cannot be denied that, at the present day, they have assumed alarming and wide-spread dimensions.

Now the Catholic Church possesses within her vast treasury special antidotes against all errors and malpractices. If men will crave after the occult and mysterious, they will find in the Catholic Church a true form of genuine Spiritism, by which man places himself in direct and personal communication with the Supreme Spirit, God the Holy Ghost Himself, Who actually comes to abide with him and by Whose influence all that is good, noble, and beautiful within the soul of man is brought out and raised to perfection, and man himself is made God-like.

Hence special devotion to the Holy Ghost, the Third Person of the most Adorable Trinity, so strongly advocated and recommended by His Holiness, the Sovereign Pontiff, Leo XIII, is most opportune; and it is a healthy sign of the times to notice that his fatherly advice has not been left unheeded.

In these pages, a series of instructions and devotions is offered to the Faithful to enable them to acquire and practice genuine devotion to the Holy Ghost.

May this little book become a powerful means of making the Spirit of Divine Love ever more known, loved, and adored by all men on earth. Amen.

Part First

I. God the Father

1. God the Father made you

God made you what you are—a human being, "a little less than the angels." He "crowned you with glory and honor, set you over the works of His hands, and subjected all things under your feet." Yet this earth is not a lasting abode. You are but a pilgrim here. Heaven is to be your true home. It is there you shall see your God "face to face," and be happy with Him for evermore.

2. God made you for Himself

God made you "to His own image and likeness," and destined you for union with Himself; a union, to commence already here, but to be perfected in heaven; a union, far beyond the loftiest conceptions and aspirations of any created being; a union, altogether above nature; a union, which will make you "a partaker of the Divine Nature," give you to live of the life of God Himself, and share in His own eternal glory and blessedness.

"You shall be as gods," was after all not said without a deep foundation of truth.

3. God made you to be His child

To bring about this blissful union, God wills to raise you up far above your natural condition—to make you, by adoption, what His own Divine Son is to Him by nature, "a beloved son, well pleasing to Him;" so that, enjoying this privilege of sonship, and living as becomes a son and child of God, you may, with full confidence, look forward to the inheritance of your "Father Who is in heaven."

4. God adopts you through His Son made man

As God made all things through His Eternal Word, "without Whom was made nothing that was made," so also has He been pleased that through the same Eternal Word you should be enabled to attain the sublime destiny for which you were created. Therefore, did the Father send on earth His Son, that, "the Word being made flesh," through Him all flesh should be saved.

II. God the Son

1. God the Son redeemed you

"The Word was made flesh, and dwelt amongst us." Why this Incarnation of the Son of God? For your sake.

Though God, He became a man like unto yourself, in order that you, a mere man, might become like unto Him, and, through Him, like unto God. He came to draw you to Himself. From heaven He descended upon earth, to lift you up from earth to heaven.

But there was an obstacle in the way of His merciful design in your behalf—an obstacle which no created power could remove. It was sin. "By one man sin entered into the world." And by that sin you were made a slave of Satan, doomed to death and endless misery, and shut out forever from heaven. What did Christ do? He, the Son of God, made man, took upon Himself that sin, and the sins of all men, in order to atone for them, and blot them out. He, the "Lamb of God, took away the sins of the world." He did so by His sufferings and death. "He was wounded for our iniquities, He was bruised for our sins, and by His bruises we are healed." And thus did He become our Redeemer. And by His Passion and the painful sacrifice of His life, He not only put away the sins which prevented your union with God, but also merited for you all the means necessary to enable you to effect that happy union.

2. Jesus Christ—the Way, the Truth and the Life

By His example, Jesus Christ traced out the right road from earth to heaven. If you walk in His footsteps, you will assuredly reach one day your true home above. He is "the Way."

By His teaching, He made known all truth necessary for salvation. If you believe in His word, it "will enlighten you," and prove "a lamp to your feet and a light to your paths." He is "the Truth."

By His death, He obtained for you that sublime gift of divine grace, which is the spiritual life of your soul. If you soul be adorned with it, through life and in death, then will you "live unto God," in time and in eternity. He is "the Life."

3. Jesus Christ entrusted the Means of Salvation to His Church

In order to put the means of salvation within easy reach of you, Jesus Christ founded His Church, and built it upon a solid foundation, even upon a rock, so that "the gates of hell itself should never prevail against it." This Church He endowed with His own divine Power and Authority, and enriched with all the treasures of His grace and truth, so that it might teach you without error, administer unto you the life-giving Sacraments, and direct you safely and securely on the road to heaven.

4. The Means of Salvation are applied to you by the Holy Ghost

All that Jesus Christ did, however, was but a preparation for your individual sanctification and salvation.

It was through the agency of the Third Person of the Blessed Trinity, that the work was to be completed and perfected. Therefore was the Holy Ghost sent to you from above by the Father and the Son.

III. God the Holy Ghost

1. God the Holy Ghost sanctifies you

God's Holy Spirit came upon you for the first time in Baptism, when you were "born again of water and the Holy Ghost." It was then He actually made you a child of God, pouring forth into your soul the priceless gift of sanctifying grace, merited for you by Jesus Christ. And having made you a child of God, He also provided you with the necessary helps to enable you to conduct yourself as such, and by due obedience and submission to His will, to reach His home in heaven.

2. The Holy Ghost abides within you

When the Holy Spirit of God first came to you, He came to stay and abide with you forever. He took complete possession of your soul, replenishing it with His choicest gifts, especially with His love and charity. Your heart became His dwelling-place and tabernacle, your very body His living temple; your whole being was sanctified by His divine presence within you.

3. The Holy Ghost is the Bond of Union between you and God

As the Holy Ghost is the substantial bond of union between the Father and the Son, so is He also, through His personal in-dwelling in your soul, the bond of union between God and yourself. And having once established that ineffable union and divine alliance, He leaves nothing undone to preserve and strengthen it, till at length it attains its full measure of perfection in heaven. By the secret workings of His grace in your heart, and by the outward ministrations of the church, of which He Himself is the life-giving principle, He labors unceasingly to keep you ever more closely united to God.

4. The Holy Ghost casts off no one

Should you, at any time, have the misfortune to sever that union by grievous sin, and so expel the Good Spirit from His dwelling-place within you; yet, He will not altogether forsake you, nor entirely give you up into the hands of your enemies. Just as a bird that is wantonly driven away from its nest, keeps fluttering and flying about in the near vicinity, ready to at once return to its home, on the departure of the unfriendly hand that disturbed it; so will this heavenly Dove, even when most unkindly offended by you, and banished from your soul, still keep hovering around, in the hope of speedily regaining possession of His rightful abode. The still voice of His grace will whisper to you of your soul's sad condition, bring home to you your guilt, and urge you to sorrow and repentance. And at the first sign of a surrender on your part—of a humble acknowledgment of your waywardness and of a desire for reconciliation— this divine Dove will swiftly approach you, return to you sweetly on the wings of love, and make you His own once more, giving back to you all that you had lost through sin.

5. The Holy Ghost is the Fount of Life and Strength

The Divine Spirit is the source and origin of all that is good within you. He it is Who enables you to see things in their true light, and take a correct view of them; to think, and speak, and act at all times in a right way. Every pious thought your mind conceives; every holy desire and aspiration your heart elicits; every profitable word that passes your lips; every noble and meritorious action that beautifies your life—all these come from the Holy Ghost, and through Him receive their increase, their maturity, and their perfection.

It is He Who enables you to pray in a manner pleasing to heaven and beneficial to yourself; to hear the word of God, so as to keep it; to so worthily approach the sacraments as to be ready to suffer everything, even death itself, if needs be, rather than betray your faith and religion.

In a word, it is the Holy Ghost Who, by His grace, enlightens you to know what is good and virtuous, and strengthens you to act in accordance with that knowledge, by avoiding all that is evil, and shunning every sinful and vicious practice.

6. The Holy Ghost is your Comforter

The Holy Ghost, "the God of all comfort," stands by you during the whole course of your mortal career, and after death, until you are safe in your Father's home. When temptation assails and wearies you, He is there to lend a helping hand, to bear you up, lest you become downcast and despondent, and fall away. In times of sorrow and sadness, He pours into your grief-stricken soul the balm of His heavenly consolation. In the midst of the troubles, trials and contradictions of life, He mitigates and sweetens your sufferings by the unction of His grace, and fills you with joy and gladness. At any time that your cross is heavier than usual, and you feel weak and faint, and are ready to sink beneath the burden, then, by holding up to your vision the glory that awaits you at your journey's end, He raises your drooping spirits and cheers you on to walk patiently in the footsteps of Jesus Christ. When death is at hand He shields you against the last attacks of the Evil One, and smooths your passage to eternity. And should divine Justice demand that your soul, when freed from its body of flesh, be, for a time, confined to the prison-house of fire, "until you pay the last farthing," even there will this Sweet Spirit be with you, to soothe the ardor of the torturing flame, and comfort you in your affliction. And He will also inspire charitable souls on earth to think of you, and show their sympathy and compassion, and bring succor and relief to you in your distress. And when at length your soul shall be thoroughly cleansed of all its sins and imperfections, and ready to go to heaven, it is this same Spirit of Love that will bear you aloft, present you to your Father's embrace, and place you on your throne of glory. And, finally, it is He, too, Who will clothe you again on the last day with your body—a body glorious and impassible, to shine forever as one of Christ's saints in His own blessed kingdom above.

7. God is to be glorified for all He has done for you

Give, then, glory to God for all He has done for you! Glory to the Father, Who made you for Heaven! Glory to the Son, Who redeemed you in order to put you on the right road to heaven! Glory to the Holy Ghost, Who sanctifies you by applying to your soul the merits of the Redemption purchased for you, and brings you to your Father Who is in heaven.

8. The Holy Ghost to be glorified in an especial manner

On the part of God, each of the Three Divine Persons loves you alike with a love that is infinite and eternal. Yet, as you, on your part, owe everything, immediately and directly, to the mysterious operations of the Third Person of the Blessed Trinity, it is but right that you should honor Him with a special tribute of adoration, thanksgiving and love. To put this before you in as clear a light as possible, it will be well to consider somewhat more at large the work of the Divine Spirit.

IV. THE HOLY GHOST AND JESUS CHRIST

1. Jesus Christ given by the Holy Ghost

Jesus Christ is your Savior. But who has given you this Savior? It was the Holy Ghost.

2. The World prepared for the coming of the Redeemer by the Holy Ghost

It was God the Holy Ghost Who prepared the world for the coming of the Divine Redeemer. He it was Who preserved intact the knowledge of the true, living God among His chosen people, in spite of the blindness and corruption which surrounded them. He it was Who taught the Patriarchs, Who spoke by the mouth of the Prophets, Who moved and guided the pen of the Sacred Writers, and Who filled the hearts of the just with an ardent longing for the speedy advent of the promised Messias.

3. The Mother of the Redeemer prepared by the Holy Ghost

It was the Holy Ghost Who singled out from among all the daughters of Eve, Mary, who "is blessed among women," and of whom was to be born Christ the Savior. He it was Who prepared her so as to be a worthy mother of the Son of God, the Redeemer of mankind. This He did by bestowing upon her that singular gift, the Immaculate Conception, by which He preserved Her from contracting the stain of original guilt, replenished her with grace from the very first moment of her existence, and guarded her, likewise, from the least taint or stain of actual sin.

4. The Mystery of the Incarnation accomplished by the Holy Ghost

It was through the Holy Ghost that "the Word was made Flesh." He it was Who "overshadowed" Mary and Who, by a most mysterious operation, fashioned within her the most Sacred Manhood of Jesus Christ.

5. The Sacred Manhood of Jesus endowed with the gifts of the Holy Ghost

It was the Holy Ghost Who adorned the Sacred Manhood of Jesus Christ with the choicest gifts of nature and of grace, "anointing Him with the oil of gladness above his fellows;" so that "He was beautiful above the sons of men," and "advanced in wisdom, and age, and grace, with God and men," according to the prophecy of Isaias: "The Spirit of the Lord shall rest upon Him."

6. The Divinity of Jesus Christ manifested by the Holy Ghost

It was the Holy Ghost Who bore witness to the Divine Nature and mission of Jesus Christ. He it was Who inspired with a most lively faith, not only the lowly shepherds on the mountain-side of Bethlehem, but also the Wise Men from the East; so that they humbly adored as their God, Him Whom they beheld lying in the manger as a new-born babe. He it was Who made known the Divine Character of the Holy Child to aged Simeon and the devout Anna, on the occasion of His being brought to the Temple to be presented to the Lord. He it was Who, in the visible form of a dove, publicly proclaimed His divinity. He it was by Whose power the apostles, at the mere bidding of Jesus, left all things and followed Him, believing Him to be the true Messias and the Son of God. He it was Who afterward

confirmed them in the faith, and enabled them, by their
preaching, to convert the whole world to the gospel of
their Divine Master.

7. Jesus Christ guided in all His actions by the Holy Ghost

It was the Holy Ghost Who directed every move, and
guided every step, of Jesus. He it was Who bade Him
"be about His Father's business," when as a boy of
twelve He remained in the Temple, and showed forth
His hidden wisdom and learning, in such a way as to
fill with wonder and admiration the Doctors of the
Law, and Mary and Joseph also. He it was by Whom
Jesus was led into the desert, to prepare Himself for
His public life by prayer, fasting and retirement; and by
Whose inspired word He overcame the attacks of Satan
when tempted by him in the wilderness. And during
the three years of His Sacred Ministry, "the Spirit of the
Lord was upon Him" in a special manner, "to preach to
the meek, to heal the contrite of heart, and to preach
a release to the captives." It was finally "by the Holy
Ghost that Christ offered Himself unspotted to God"
and consummated the great Sacrifice upon the Cross.
It was the same "Spirit that raised up Jesus from the
dead," and made Him ascend on high, "to sit at the
right hand of the Father, from whence He shall come
to judge the living and the dead." In a word, all the

actions of Jesus Christ were performed in and by the Holy Ghost.

8. Jesus Christ still on earth through the operation of the Holy Ghost

It is by the grace of the Holy Ghost that Jesus Christ even now reigns in the hearts of millions of men on earth, and will reign to the end of time. It is by the power of the Holy Ghost that Jesus Christ even now personally abides in our midst through His Sacramental Presence in the Holy Eucharist, to be daily offered in sacrifice upon the altar, and to be given as food for the spiritual refreshment of the soul.

V. The Holy Ghost and the Church

1. The Mission of Jesus Christ perpetuated by His Church

Jesus Christ came on earth "to enlighten every man that cometh into the world;" to give life "so that all might have it, and have it more abundantly;" to be "the Good Shepherd whose voice all men should hear and obey." But you have never seen our Lord or heard His voice. How, then, does He enlighten you, how give life to you, how guide you? This He does, as you know, by the ministry of His Church, established by Him for the express purpose of continuing His mission on earth all days, even to the end of time. Her teaching enlightens you; her sacraments give you life; her authority is your guide.

2. The Church owes her existence to the Holy Ghost

If it be through the ministration of the Church that you can have access to the Merits of your Divine Redeemer, it may be asked, how was the Church herself brought into existence? The answer is, by the Holy Ghost. As at the creation of man, "God breathed into his face the breath of life, and man became a living soul," so, on the day of Pentecost, God the Father and the Son breathed down from heaven the Holy Ghost; and "a sound was heard as that of a mighty wind;" and in that mighty wind the Holy Ghost descended and filled the hearts of the Apostles and Disciples. Thus the Church of God was quickened into existence by the Holy Ghost; so that He is the life-giver, nay, the very life and soul of the Church.

3. The Church extended and preserved by the Holy Ghost

It was the Holy Ghost Who enabled the Apostles boldly to appear before the multitudes, and fearlessly to announce "Christ, and Him Crucified" to Jew and

Gentile, so as even to brave every danger, and in the end
to seal their mission with their life's blood. He it was
Who so blessed their preaching that, in it short time,
"their sound had gone into all the earth and their words
unto the ends of the whole world," and that thousands
upon thousands bowed to the name of Jesus, and gladly
shed their blood in testimony to their faith. He it is
Who has ever preserved the church in existence, in spite
of the most powerful opposition raised against her, by
enemies both from within and from without. Persecu-
tions swept over the Church; heresies sprang up; schisms
arose; but by the power of the Holy Ghost, she came
forth from every conflict more vigorous than ever, even
at times when, humanly speaking, she seemed doomed
to sink and perish.

4. The Church sanctified and glorified by the Holy Ghost

It is the Holy Ghost Who has at all times raised up
in the Church those great luminaries of learning and
prodigies of holiness who command the respect and
challenge the veneration of all generations.

It is to Him that martyrs owe their invincible courage and fortitude, Confessors their patience and con-
stancy in virtue, Virgins their purity and chastity.

It is He Who keeps the church from the least shadow
of error, so as to make her the very "pillar and ground of
the truth." He it is Who imparts to the Sovereign Pontiff,

Christ's Vicar on earth, the gift of personal infallibility, so as to make him the living mouthpiece of the Spirit of Truth. He it is Who gives Divine Authority to Pontiffs and Priests, so that it can be said that "he who heareth them, heareth Christ Himself." He it is Who calls them to the Sacred Ministry, and enables them to perform the arduous duties of their sublime vocation, so that they are ever ready to lay down their very lives for their flocks, as indeed great numbers have done.

It is He Who gives thousands of heroic souls a special call to the Religious State, where they may lead a higher and more perfect life, by stripping themselves of all earthly goods, and following Christ more closely, devoting all their time and energy to the service of God and the interests of their fellow men.

It is He Who produces in the hearts of the faithful at large the fruits of every Christian virtue, enabling them to lead blameless lives in the midst of a corrupt world, and to die peacefully in the Lord.

VI. The Holy Ghost and the Means of Salvation

1. To the Holy Ghost you owe the gift of Divine Adoption

If you would save your soul you must be the child of God your Father, Who is in heaven. But who makes you a child of God, and who assures you of the Divine adoption but the Holy Ghost? "whereby you cry, Abba, Father!"

2. The Holy Ghost makes you like unto Jesus, the Son of God

If you would save your soul you must "be made conformable to the image of the Son of God." But who produces within you this Divine likeness, if not the Holy Ghost, Who applies to your soul the infinite merits of Jesus Christ, and thus enables you to "put on Christ" Himself!

3. The Holy Ghost your stay and support

If you would save your soul you must look on this earth as a place of exile, where you are to labor, to suffer and to die, in preparation for your journey to a better land. But who save the Holy Ghost will enable you to prepare yourself properly for eternity, since He it is Who is given to you to sustain you whilst in this valley of tears, and is "to help your infirmity!"

4. To the Holy Ghost you owe the gift of prayer

If you would save your soul you must pray. But how can you pray aright; nay, how do you even "know what you should pray for," except by the Holy Ghost, "Who Himself asketh for you with unspeakable groanings!"

5. The Holy Ghost imparts strength to do penance

If you would save your soul you must practice self-denial. But who enables you to "mortify the deeds of the flesh," "chastise your body and bring it into subjection," and keep a strict guard over your senses and appetites, except the Spirit of God, Who gives power to your spirit to "resist the allurements of the flesh?"

6. Without the aid of the Holy Ghost you cannot do good nor avoid evil

If you would save your soul you must practice virtue and shun sin. But who inspires you with good and holy thoughts, who assists you in the performance of good actions, and who crowns your good works with an everlasting reward? Who fills your soul with hatred of sin, and helps you to flee from it as from a poisonous serpent? Who aids you to rise again and again when you are so unfortunate as to fall? It is the Holy Ghost Who does all this.

7. The outward means of Salvation, administered by the Church made efficacious by the Holy Ghost

If you would save your soul, you must employ, as far as you possibly can, the outward means of salvation placed at your disposal by the Church. You must believe her teaching, receive her Sacraments and obey

her authority. But who implants within your soul the
gift of faith? Who prepares your soul for a worthy reception of the Sacraments? Who applies to you internally
the fruits of the Sacraments? Who preserves within your
soul the salutary effects of the Sacraments? Who makes
you a docile and obedient member of God's Church?
Behold, all this is done by the Holy Ghost dwelling
within you.

8. The Holy Ghost enables you to respect and obey law and authority

If you would save your soul, you must keep the law;
you must observe the commandments of God, obey the
precepts of the Church and submit to lawful authority.
But who gives you that humble and submissive heart to
be faithful in the discharge of your duties on all occasions, in matters both great and small, unless the Holy
Ghost, Who enlightens your mind to know and understand what is to be done, and strengthens your will to
do it?

9. Extraordinary means of Salvation made efficacious by the Holy Ghost

To enable you to save your soul more easily, the
Church puts within your reach quite a number of
extraordinary means of sanctification. Her Sacred Rites
and ceremonies, for instance, with their beautiful,

symbolical meanings; her grand and impressive liturgy; her exorcisms to counteract and defeat the power of the evil one; the blessing of various objects, to obtain the special protection of God and of His Saints; her religious confraternities and sodalities to promote union and charity amongst her members; her inexhaustible treasury of beautiful and touching devotions—those especially having reference to our Blessed Lord, His Holy Mother, the Angels and Saints, and the Faithful Departed—through all these does the Church convey to you many spiritual benefits and helps to salvation. She offers them to you as a fruitful source of countless blessings, for time and for eternity. But to whom do they really owe their existence and their sanctifying virtue? To the Holy Ghost.

VII. THE CHURCH THE ORDINARY CHANNEL BY WHICH THE HOLY GHOST DISPENSES HIS GRACES AND GIFTS

1. The Work of the Holy Ghost universal

The Holy Ghost is the Sanctifier of all men, no matter when or where they lived or shall live—no matter whether before or after the coming of Jesus Christ— whether within the visible pale of the church or outside it. Whenever, therefore, at any time, or in any place, men are sanctified, the work is done by the Holy Ghost. From the first human pair in Paradise to the last human being that shall be born into the world, no man ever did, or could, or shall receive grace but by the Holy Ghost.

2. The Work of the Holy Ghost different as to times and circumstances

Although the work of the Holy Ghost is universal, yet there are differences of operation according to times and circumstances. Before the coming of Jesus Christ, God was, indeed, "a hidden God;" and hence the work of sanctifying the souls of men was carried on by the Spirit of God, in a hidden, silent and mysterious manner.

But after the coming of Jesus Christ, when God Himself, the author of grace, had become visible, by means of the Incarnation, grace itself, also, was in a manner made visible and tangible by means of the Sacraments instituted by Jesus Christ to produce it in our hearts. And since Jesus Christ entrusted the Sacraments to His Church, it follows that they are the ordinary channels through which the Holy Ghost now dispenses His gifts and graces; so that, unless we have recourse to them, we shall not receive the graces of God's Holy Spirit. Christ Himself has so willed and ordained it.

3. The Action of the Holy Ghost not confined to the Visible Church

The operations of the Holy Ghost, however, are not restricted to those who are visibly within the pale of the Church. He works in the souls of those who are without, as well as of those who are within. Some are outside the Church through no fault of theirs. And if they act at all times according to their lights, according to their knowledge of right and wrong, and according to the dictates of their conscience, with a good and sincere heart before God, they will assuredly get to heaven, and save their soul. In what way the Holy Ghost sanctifies them is not known; but He does sanctify them, truly and efficaciously, if they but faithfully cooperate with the graces and helps He grants to them. Verily, "hath the Spirit of the Lord filled the whole earth" . . . "dividing His gifts to every one as He will."

On the day of Pentecost the Holy Ghost came down in a visible and stupendous manner upon the Apostles, Disciples and others assembled together, in expectation of that wonderful event. Ever since that day, on which He inaugurated His special mission to the Church of God, He has been pouring out His gifts and favors upon the hearts of the Faithful, on a larger and more diversified scale than ever before; He has been communicating them to us in greater fullness and variety. Thus the work of salvation has been rendered much easier. If the Sacraments, for instance, are duly administered and worthily received, they infallibly produce the grace which they signify; they restore, or increase, the spiritual life of the soul, rendering it more vigorous and strong to do its duty to God; and thus they afford facilities for salvation that are not to be found outside of the Church.

4. The Operations of the Holy Ghost not absolutely dependent on the Sacraments

Although the Church is bound to administer the Sacraments, and you, as a child of the Church, cannot expect God's grace without having recourse to these outward means of sanctification established by Christ, yet in some cases the full benefit of a Sacrament may be obtained without the Sacrament itself being received. The Holy Ghost may produce its effect in the soul quite independently of its actual administration. Some one, for instance, wants to be baptized; but there is no person to perform the sacred rite. In this case the earnest desire for the Sacrament, accompanied with a genuine sorrow for sin, will supply the place of Baptism by water, and justify him before God, and render him fit for heaven. In like manner, if any one not yet baptized suffer martyrdom for the faith of Jesus Christ, this sacrifice of his life, the strongest proof of love that he can give will serve instead of Baptism to wash away his sins.

He is baptized in his blood. Again, as regards the Sacrament of Penance, one may not find a priest to hear his confession and give him absolution, but an act of perfect contrition, joined with a sincere desire to approach the Sacrament, will compensate for its actual reception, and take away his sins, and open heaven to him if he die. In these several instances, in which the real reception of the Sacrament is rendered impossible, we see the Holy Spirit sanctifying the soul without the ordained means of grace which He usually employs for that purpose. And there is no doubt that He may enlighten and sanctify souls and direct them in the way of salvation in a more extraordinary manner still; for, being God, He is necessarily independent and cannot absolutely be tied down to outward observances. "The Spirit breatheth where He will."

5. Obedience to the Church a sure test of being led by the Spirit of God

As we have seen, it is, strictly speaking, possible to be saved without all, or even any, of the church's ministrations. Do not, however, allow yourself to be deceived on this point—to be carried away by vain and absurd expectations.

Do not imagine, for instance, that the Holy Ghost is going to favor you with any private revelation in matters of Faith, or communicate Himself to your soul in some miraculous manner, or take you under His special personal guidance. All this would be both foolish and sinful. For you have the infallible voice of the Church to teach you all truth; her Sacraments to enrich you with grace; her divine authority to lead and direct you aright. If you reject the Church's teaching, refuse her Sacraments, resist her authority, under the pretense of a special impulse and instruction from the Spirit of God, you clearly show that you are under the influence of quite another spirit. No one is led by the Holy Ghost, but who is loyal and submissive to the Church and her Supreme Head on earth, the Sovereign Pontiff. For "whosoever despises the Church despises Christ;" and he who despises Christ can assuredly have no partnership with His Divine Spirit.

VIII. Special Devotion to the Holy Ghost

1. What it means

It will be well for you, now and again, to consider all you owe to the Holy Ghost. If you do this seriously and with due reflection, you cannot fail to be animated with a holy desire to cultivate a special devotion to His Divine Person.

You will offer Him a special tribute of praise and adoration, as being your God—the God of your whole being. You will love Him with all your heart's sincerest love; for He is the Spirit of charity—Love itself. You will pay Him the homage of most heartfelt gratitude for the constant, unwearied kindness He has ever shown towards you. You will pray to Him in a most special manner, since He is your Comforter and Helper in every sorrow and need.

You will think of Him often. You will be ever mindful of His loving and patient indwelling within you. You will endeavor to follow His Divine Inspirations, by which He guides you internally. You will cheerfully obey all lawful authority, by which He guides you externally. You will take heed lest you "grieve Him" by willful neglect, by sloth or lukewarmness, or "extinguish" the fire of His Divine Love within you, by yielding to grievous sin. You will take care to be diligent in His Divine service. You will faithfully perform some devout exercises in His honor. You will not fail to make reparation for the slights and insults offered to His Divine Majesty by the sons of men.

Doing this, you will cultivate special devotion to the Holy Ghost.

2. What special devotion to the Holy Ghost will do

It is the Holy Ghost Who made you a child of God and brother of Jesus Christ. Special devotion to Him will make you realize this heaven-born dignity more and more, and urge you on to conduct yourself in a manner befitting a child of God and a brother of Jesus Christ.

It is the Holy Ghost Who made you a member of God's true Church. Special devotion to Him will make you value the grand privilege of belonging to the one, true Fold, and induce you to live and die as a worthy and zealous member of Christ's flock.

It is the Holy Ghost Who clothes your soul with the garment of sanctifying grace. Special devotion to Him will make you love and esteem this priceless treasure above all things, employ all means to preserve and increase it, shun everything that would weaken or destroy it, do all to recover it when lost.

It is the Holy Ghost Who continually aids you with the gift of actual grace. Special devotion to Him will encourage you on to be more mindful of your weaknesses and miseries, to lean upon Him for continued assistance, to call upon Him in every need.

It is the Holy Ghost Who implanted in your soul the supernatural habits of faith, hope and charity, and sowed therein the seed of every other virtue. Special devotion to Him will give you a stronger faith, a firmer hope and a more ardent charity and likewise help you to acquire and practice every virtue according to your station in life.

The Holy Ghost is in a particular manner the Spirit

of Truth. Special devotion to Him will guard you against indifference in matters of Religion, so prevalent in these days, and preserve you from heresy and infidelity.

The Holy Ghost has consecrated and sanctified your very body, for in it He dwells as in His temple. Special devotion to Him will make you reverence and respect your own body as well as the bodies of others, as being something sacred, and will preserve you from those shameful and degrading vices of intemperance and impurity by which men defile their bodies as well as their souls.

It is the Holy Ghost Who bestows upon you His seven great gifts. Special devotion to Him will make you understand them better and employ them more faithfully.

His gift of wisdom will protect and shield your soul against foolishness; His gift of Understanding, against dullness of mind; His gift of Counsel, against rashness; His gift of Knowledge, against ignorance; His gift of Fortitude, against faint-heartedness; His gift of Piety, against hardness of heart; His gift of the Fear of the Lord, against pride and presumption.

Being diligent in using these Divine Gifts, you will produce in the garden of your soul the most delightful fruits of the Holy Ghost: charity, as an effect of wisdom; peace, as an effect of understanding; joy, as an effect of knowledge; benignity and goodness as an effect of

counsel; patience and longanimity, as an effect of fortitude; faith and mildness, as an effect of piety; modesty,
continency and chastity, as an effect of the fear of the
Lord.

3. Special marks of the true servant of the Holy Ghost

Special devotion to the Holy Ghost will imprint particular marks upon you.

Modesty will accompany all your looks, words, and
actions. A sweet gravity will regulate all the movements of your body. Purity, discretion and kindness will
prompt your words. You will be temperate in food and
drink. Patience, and even joy, will be yours in the midst
of sufferings and tribulations. Towards your superiors,
you will ever have a ready will to obey and submit;
towards your inferiors you will be kind and conde-
scending; towards your equals, humble and loving. You
will be filled with zeal for God's greater honor and glory,
and the salvation of souls. You will be all on fire to promote the interests of Jesus Christ and of His Church.
You will be loyally devoted to the See of Peter. You will
have a tender love for the Person of Jesus in the most
Blessed Sacrament of the Altar, and a filial devotion to
Mary Immaculate. You will be diligent and fervent in
the exercise of Divine worship. You will enjoy fervor
and recollection at prayer. You will love to assist at Holy

Mass, and frequent the Sacraments. You will be constant in all good works. You will persevere in God's love, die in His friendship, and be especially rewarded in His blessed Kingdom for ever.

Devotion to the Holy Ghost may be called a special sign of election in the latter days of the world according to the testimony of St. Jude: "In the last time, there will come mockers, walking according to their own desires in ungodliness. These are they, separating themselves, having not the spirit. But you, my beloved, building yourselves upon your most holy faith, praying in the Holy Ghost, keep yourselves in the love of God, waiting for the mercy of our Lord Jesus Christ unto life everlasting."

4. Exhortation to practice special devotion to the Holy Ghost

Do not hesitate to take up, and practice, special devotion to the Holy Ghost. In this, there is proposed to you nothing new or strange. Devotion to the Holy Ghost has, in fact, been practiced in the Church from the beginning; nay, her very foundation may be called an effect of this devotion, the Apostles and Disciples being gathered together in one place at the command of their Divine Master, to pray for the coming of the promised Paraclete.

True, this devotion is utterly unknown to the world;

but so it always was, and will be. It is but slightly known to the tepid and indifferent, much to their own cost. But it has ever been practiced, in some shape or form, by the fervent, as may be seen at a glance from the lives of all the great servants of God.

This devotion, like every other, will not be without its adversaries. Satan and his crew will rise against it; for "they hate the light and love the darkness." The flesh and its lusts will chafe against it; for its teeth are set on edge by the fruits of the Spirit, especially modesty, chastity, and continency. The world and its votaries will storm against it; for it is ruled by the spirit of darkness and infidelity, the spirit of selfish greed and avarice, the spirit of lust and immorality. False Christians, too, will oppose it. Devotees will mar it through indiscreet zeal. Zealots will rise to put it down as something novel, or cause it to be repressed by those in authority. Yet genuine devotion to the Divine Spirit is bound to flourish in spite of all opposition, making those who practice it diligent in the discharge of their duties, respectful and obedient to their superiors; producing a corrective sorrow in the hearts of true penitents, and prudent zeal in the hearts of the fervent; uniting all in the sweet bond of peace, in loyal submission to him who, as the mouthpiece of the Holy Ghost and Vicar of Christ, rules and governs the Church in the See of Peter.

IX. The Holy Ghost and the Priesthood

1. Call to the Sacred Priesthood a special grace of the Holy Ghost

"You are a priest forever, according to the order of Melchisedech." But to whom do you owe this exalted dignity? Who first inspired you with the thought of consecrating yourself to God's service in the Sacred Priesthood? Who encouraged and aided you to follow this Divine call, until that solemn moment when the words were addressed to you: "Receive the Holy Ghost," and when you rose with the indelible mark of the Eternal Priesthood stamped upon your soul? And who has ever since guided, strengthened, and comforted you in the discharge of the arduous duties of the Sacred Ministry? No other than the Holy Ghost, Who has communicated Himself to you in a very special manner to make you a priest of the Most High.

2. The dignity of the Priesthood closely resembles that of the Divine Maternity

Oh! who can ever fathom the sublime dignity of the priesthood! Great indeed beyond conception is Mary's dignity, as Mother of the Eternal Son of God made man. But that of the priest closely approaches hers. Through Mary's instrumentality, Jesus Christ, the Redeemer was given to men. Through the instrumentality of the priest the same Savior is born, so, to speak, afresh, each day, sacramentally upon the Altar, and spiritually, in the hearts of the faithful. Mary enjoyed the privilege of carrying in her arms the Son of God, made man; the priest tremblingly holds in his hands each day the same Son of God made man, hidden under the lowly forms of bread and wine, and offers Him in sacrifice to God, for the living and the dead, and distributes Him as food, for the spiritual refreshment of the soul. And in either case, the mystery is performed by the operation of the Holy Ghost. As the Holy Ghost overshadowed Mary, and produced within her the Sacred Humanity of Jesus Christ, so He overshadows the priest, and makes him the instrument of reproducing Jesus Christ in the Blessed Sacrament of the Altar and in the hearts of the faithful!

3. The office of the Priesthood a communication of the office of the Holy Ghost

The Holy Ghost, to a certain extent, communicates to the priest His own Divine Office. It is the office of the Holy Ghost to apply to the souls of men the infinite merits of Jesus Christ; yet this He ordinarily does through the instrumentality of the priest by the administration of the Sacraments. It is the office of the Holy Ghost to enlighten, guide, and safeguard the souls of men on the road to heaven; but this, again, He ordinarily does through the instrumentality of the priest, who is divinely appointed to direct and govern men in all matters relating to the eternal welfare of their immortal souls. It is the office of the Holy Ghost to be in a special manner the Paraclete, the Comforter, to gladden the souls of men in their sojourn through this valley of tears. And what is the priest of God, but another Paraclete; a true comforter, making known the glad tidings of salvation; dispensing the sweet consolations of Religion to all who are weighed down with sin and sorrow, who are harassed with doubt and fear, and afflicted with the troubles and misfortunes of this life!

The outpouring of the gifts of the Holy Ghost in the soul of the priest is so abundant, that the Holy Ghost may in all truth be said to communicate Himself entirely to the priest with the fullness of His treasures, giving him power to produce and distribute divine grace in the souls of men, and thus beget them to a new life, even to life everlasting in the Kingdom of heaven.

4. The Priest another Christ by the power of the Holy Ghost

The priesthood was instituted by Jesus Christ to continue His Divine Mission on earth even to the end of time. The priest, therefore, represents on earth the Person of Jesus Christ, so that He could, in truth, say to His priests: "He that heareth you, heareth me." The priest is, in fact, another Christ, and this by the power of the Holy Ghost; so that each priest can apply to himself the words of the Prophet, written concerning the Divine Redeemer: "The Spirit of the Lord is upon me, because the Lord hath anointed me. He hath sent me to preach to the meek, to heal the contrite of heart, to preach a release to the captives and deliverance to them that are shut up; to proclaim the acceptable year of the Lord, and the day of vengeance of our God; to comfort all that mourn."

5. Devotion to the Holy Ghost a great help to the Priest and his people

Blessed the priest whose soul is awake to the special operation of the Holy Ghost within him, and whose heart is all on fire with special devotion for His Divine Person, on account of the extraordinary gifts and favors received from Him; for he will more fully recognize his exalted dignity; he will labor more zealously and diligently in the vineyard of the Lord; and his efforts will not fail to be crowned with a more plentiful harvest of souls and a more abundant reward for himself.

Blessed the priest, in whose flock the Spirit of God is known, honored and loved in a special manner. The more the Holy Ghost is known by the faithful, the more shall they increase in faith and piety. The more the Holy Ghost is honored and invoked by them, the better will they understand the preaching of the Gospel, and the more readily obey its precepts. The more the Holy Ghost is loved by them, the greater will be their zeal for God's greater glory and the spread of His Divine Kingdom.

X. The Holy Ghost and Religious Orders

1. Call to the Religious State a special grace of the Holy Ghost

It is to the soul of every Religious that these words of the Holy Ghost may be applied in a special manner: "Behold, I will allure her, and I will lead her into the wilderness; and I will speak to her heart."

You who are a Religious, tell me, who "allured" you away from the vanities of a deceitful world? Who "led" you to your abode of sweet seclusion and retirement? Who first "spoke to your heart" of the peaceful service of God in the cloister? Who encouraged and strengthened you to "leave all things and follow Christ?" Who enabled you to consummate the sacrifice, when by the three vows of poverty, chastity, and obedience, you made of yourself a whole-burnt offering, and fastened yourself, so to speak, with Jesus to the cross? Who has ever since that moment enabled you to be faithful to the solemn promises you then made, and to be diligent in the discharge of the sublime duties of your noble calling? Who still aids you to lead that life of prayer and recollection, so necessary to you? Who is the source and fount of the interior life you now lead—a life utterly unknown to the lovers of the world? Who gives you strength to practice the virtues befitting your exalted state? Who encourages and comforts you amidst the many trials and hardships incident to your mode of life? "I will speak, and do thou answer me." Is not all this the special work of the Holy Ghost, Who has singled you out from among the rest of mankind and called you to this blessed state of life?

2. Religious Orders the special work of the Holy Ghost

Who inspired holy men and women with the idea of establishing those numerous Religious Orders, Congregations, and Societies, which now exist in the Church of God, both as an ornament to enhance her beauty and as a bulwark to defend her against her enemies? Who aided these holy Founders to draw up the saintly rules and salutary constitutions, by which the lives of their followers were regulated and sanctified, and which in many instances have all the outward marks of a special divine inspiration? Who has raised so many Religious to the very height of perfection, and endowed them with extraordinary gifts, so that they have become renowned for holiness of life and the fame of miracles, and that "their memories are held in benediction from generation to generation?" "I will speak, and do thou answer."

Is not all this, once more, the work of the Divine Spirit, Who by these wonderful institutions proclaims Himself, in a visible and tangible manner, the Spirit of holiness and perfection!

3. Exhortation to Religious to practice devotion to the Holy Ghost

Religious soul! Can you be conscious of all you owe to the Holy Ghost, and not be moved to be devoted to Him in a very special manner? Can you feel burning within you the fire of Divine love and be heedless of Him Who is the very breath of that fire? Ah! then, let the Spirit of God reign entirely in your hearts, that He may set them yet more on fire. Fire is what you need. "I came to cast fire on earth and what will I but that it burn." Where there is fire, there is life, motion, and activity; there is true zeal and devotedness; and thence, too, will shoot forth into a cold, dismal and dreary world, flashes of light and rays of warmth, by which many a poor soul that "sitteth in darkness and the shadow of death" shall be enlightened and set on fire. Then "be you filled with the Holy Spirit" in a very special manner, so as to live, love, work and suffer for Him alone; and, being yourself filled with the Holy Spirit, make known His Love and mercy everywhere, so that all may come under the gracious empire of His Love and mercy, and that God may be ever more glorified.

XI. THE HOLY GHOST AND DEVOTION TO THE SACRED HEART OF JESUS

1. Devotion to the Holy Ghost promotes devotion to the Sacred Heart

Devotion to the Holy Ghost is a most powerful aid to foster and promote devotion to the Sacred Heart. The Sacred Heart owes everything to the direct operations of the Holy Ghost. It was the Holy Ghost Who fashioned and formed this Sacred Heart, Who filled it with grace and beauty, Who directed its movements during its mortal career on earth, nay Who directs them even now; for, in the Heart of Jesus, the Holy Ghost has taken up a permanent abode. If, therefore, you are truly devout to the Holy Ghost, you will be enabled to know and love the Sacred Heart more and more. For, who can know it better, or love it more, than the Holy Ghost?

2. Devotion to the Holy Ghost makes you truly one with the Sacred Heart

The Divine Spirit dwells ever more within the Sacred Heart of Jesus; and if He also dwells within your heart, then are you really made one heart with the Heart of Jesus. Special devotion, therefore, to the Holy Ghost is bound to so intensify that union, till it cause your heart to beat in perfect unison with the throbbings of the Sacred Heart. Then will you begin to think and judge in all matters as Jesus did; holding those things alone worthy of desire and esteem, which will bring you nearer to God and advance His glory. Then will you love and take up those things which Jesus embraced, namely, humiliation, crosses, and afflictions, so as to be ready and willing to suffer and die with Him. Then will you hate and shun the things which Jesus hated and shunned, those things, namely, which the world offers to its admirers: empty honors, deceitful riches, unlawful pleasures. Then will you become truly Christ-like, so as to exclaim with the Apostle: "I live, yet not I, but Christ liveth in me."

3. Exhortation to lovers of the Sacred Heart

Then fear not to take up this especial devotion to the Holy Ghost, since it will inflame your heart more and more with genuine love for the Sacred Heart of Jesus, and unite your heart more intimately with His—so intimately and closely, as to become all one with Him. Thus, by having special devotion to the Holy Ghost, Jesus will all the more be glorified in you, and, by you, in others—as Jesus Himself had foretold of the Holy Ghost: "He shall glorify Me."

XII. The Holy Ghost and Devotion to the Blessed Virgin Mary

Mary is inseparably united to the Holy Ghost as to her Divine Spouse. Hence, also, devotion to Mary is, of necessity, intimately connected with devotion to the Holy Ghost. The two go hand in hand; in proportion as the one increases, so does the other.

If the Holy Ghost finds in any soul genuine devotion to Mary, His Immaculate Spouse, He will be drawn to that soul more closely by the bonds of love; and in proportion to the love of that soul for Mary, so will He increase His own love for it, and enrich it with His choicest gifts and blessings.

And since true devotion to Mary is, in itself, a special grace of the Holy Ghost, do not forget frequently to implore the Divine Spirit to increase within you that tender and filial love for Mary, your heavenly Queen and Mother; and then, turning to Mary, earnestly implore her to aid you, by her intercession, to be filled daily more and more with greater love for the Holy Ghost, her Divine Spouse.

XIII. The Holy Ghost and the Souls in Purgatory

The souls whom Divine Justice detains in the cleansing flames of Purgatory, suffer most keenly; yet they enjoy, nevertheless, a holy peace and even happiness in the midst of their sufferings. And who fills them with that peace and happiness? It is the Holy Ghost, their Comforter.

Moreover, it is the Holy Ghost Who, by His Divine Revelation, has made known the state and condition of these suffering souls. He it is Who inspires men on earth to come to their assistance, and Who supplies them with the means to relieve their sufferings and hasten the day of their deliverance. Thus the Holy Ghost comforts them through others.

The more, therefore, you are filled with the Holy Ghost, the Comforter, the more readily will you come to the assistance of the poor suffering souls in Purgatory and comfort them in their distress.

XIV. THE HOLY GHOST AND THE WORKS OF MERCY

If you would find favor and mercy in God's sight, you must first yourself be kind and merciful to others. "Mercy to him that showeth mercy." And, in fact, it is according to this law of mercy that men shall be judged at the last day. For on that day, the Sovereign Judge will say to the blessed: "Come, ye blessed of my Father, possess ye the Kingdom prepared for you from the foundation of the world. For I was hungry, and you gave me to eat; I was thirsty, and you gave me to drink; I was a stranger, and you took me in; naked, and you covered me; sick, and you visited me: I was in prison, and you came to me. . . . Amen, I say unto you, as long as you did it to one of these my least brethren, you did it to Me." The wicked, on the other hand, shall be condemned, because they refused to practice these works of mercy.

Now, the Holy Ghost is the Comforter of all who are in sorrow and affliction. Hence if you are devout to the Holy Spirit, you will become, like unto Him, a Comforter to all who suffer and are in need. And thus showing mercy to others, you will secure for yourself mercy "in the evil day."

XV. The Holy Ghost and those engaged in Study or Teaching

In the Holy Ghost are contained all the treasures of knowledge and truth. If, therefore, you wish to make steady progress in learning, religious or secular, you will find great aid in practicing special devotion to God the Holy Ghost. And you who are engaged in teaching others, will obtain marvelous success, if you yourself take up this devotion, and prevail upon your pupils to embrace it. Practice, therefore, daily some devout exercise in honor of the Spirit of Truth, and He will fill you with true wisdom and understanding.

XVI. The Holy Ghost and those zealous for the spread of Faith

You who enjoy the inestimable blessings of the true Faith, should not forget that it is a duty to do what lies in you to extend these advantages to others who, as yet, are strangers to the Truth, or who, having embraced it, have fallen from it, or who "walk unworthy of their high calling." This work is not left entirely to priests. You also must do your share as far as you are able. To this end, all must employ the power of prayer, and the influence of a good example which, at times, is more efficacious than the most eloquent sermon. Some can do more. The spread of Catholic literature is a very powerful means. Kind, encouraging words, spoken at seasonable times, will also go a long way.

Yet bear in mind that whatever you may do, it is upon the Holy Ghost you must depend for success. The Apostles did not dare to appear in public, and present themselves before the multitude, until they had received the Holy Ghost on the day of Pentecost. And whatever good has ever been done by apostolic and zealous souls has been effected by the power of the same Divine Spirit.

Be zealous, then, for the spread of God's Kingdom on earth; and in order to be animated with true zeal in doing all the good you can, have recourse to the Holy Ghost in a very special manner. Invoke His aid and counsel; be fortified with the power of His might; be inflamed with the fire of His Divine Love; and be guided at all times by those whom the Holy Ghost has appointed to instruct and direct you. Then will you really become Apostles of Jesus Christ, and receive the due reward of your apostleship.

XVII. Devotion to the Holy Ghost especially commended to the Young

Youth has its own peculiar temptations. Passions are so strong; the imagination is so vivid; the world seems so attractive, and pleasure so enticing. And oh! how often is the bloom of innocence blighted, and virtue entirely wrecked!

You, therefore, who are young, ought to be especially devout to the Holy Ghost. For He alone can help you to subdue your passions, to see the deceitfulness and shallowness of all earthly riches and enjoyments, and to keep you safe from the corrupting influence of the world.

Devotion to the Holy Ghost will, in a special manner, move you to reverence, not only your souls, but also your bodies, as sacred dwelling-places of the Divine Spirit. Remember these words: "Know you not that you are the temple of God, and that the Spirit of God dwelleth in you? But if any man violate the temple of

God, him shall God destroy. For the temple of God is holy; which you are."

XVIII. Devotion to the Holy Ghost an especial antidote against the evils of the day

"There is nothing new under the sun," says the Wise Man. The evils of to-day are but the evils of yesterday. Error and vice have always existed. At various times, they assume different forms to catch the unwary and ensnare the foolish; but, at bottom, they are ever the same. Yet, at the same time, each age as it comes has its own peculiar evils. The present age is not an exception.

As to Religion, it is true that the times of harsh bigotry have passed away; but there has sprung up in its stead a spirit of total indifference which amounts to a practical denial of all Religion. People say: Why wrangle over Religious beliefs? We must take a charitable view of things. All Religions are good. None is necessary. The universal brotherhood of man is the Religion of mankind; universal benevolence its moral precept; universal prosperity its reward.

As to morality, public opinion may be pretty sound as to general moral principles; and there also may exist a certain outward show of respectability. But it is greatly to be feared that beneath this thin veil there lies hidden a deep and wide-spread corruption.

In domestic society, the sacred rights and duties of matrimony, hallowed by God and by nature, are wantonly set aside; and the results are simply appalling.

In society at large, very little justice and honesty is to be found. It is perfectly true to say that all precepts seem to have come to this: Just do as you like; only take heed not to be found out. To commit crime, seems to be crime no longer; but to be convicted of crime, is real crime.

And crime unfortunately is on the increase. Suicide, in particular, which is no doubt the greatest crime, is now more common than ever! Men have lost sight of the supernatural. Hence, when they are detected in wrong-doing, they have recourse to suicide, in order to avoid present disgrace and escape the hands of human justice; or again, when serious misfortunes or grievous sufferings fall to their lot, they seek for relief in suicide, since they have no hope in an hereafter.

But the peculiar feature of the times is that strange infatuation which has seized hold of many of attempting to break through the laws of nature, as we know them now, and to hold intercourse with the inhabitants of the unseen world. That many strange and wonderful facts occur, is beyond doubt. There are some who, in the very name of Christ, through faith and prayer—so they say—work strange cures and miracles. There are others who tell the most secret and hidden things, read the past, forecast the future, and offer advice in the most serious concerns of human life. Hypnotism, practiced by many, has resulted in the most startling facts. Some men pretend to call upon the dead and place you in direct communication with your departed friends. Others come to you in the guise of wisdom, inviting you to be initiated in occult sciences which would raise you to the condition of a sort of demigod or quasi-redeemer of the human race.

What does all this mean? That many facts are nothing but fraud and trickery is perfectly true. But that many facts must also be ascribed to the preternatural agency of evil spirits, is equally true. Yet whether they be whims or realities, this much is certain that both they who practice and they who have recourse to such things, are guilty of a very special sin and cannot draw down upon themselves or others substantial blessings. The very attempt of obtaining certain ends by the use of means which are neither ordained by nature nor sanctioned by God, is an indirect appeal to the powers of darkness.

Now against all such evils, devotion to the Holy Ghost is a most effectual antidote. For the more the Divine Spirit is known, loved, and honored by men, the more will the empire of Satan and of sin be diminished;

the more readily will men have recourse to the Spirit of God and place themselves under His safe guidance, and the more willingly will they submit, above all things, to the Divine Authority of the Catholic Church, which may rightly be called an Incarnation of the Holy Ghost. For in her, He lives and abides in the midst of men; by her, and through her, He speaks and operates in the souls of men. In the Catholic Church alone are you safeguarded against all error. In the Catholic Church alone the true principles of morality and justice are taught and defended. The Catholic Church alone has ever upheld and defended the sacred rights of matrimony. In the Catholic Church alone will you find safe protection against the snares and deception of the evil spirit and his agents. Even if you seek for miracles and prophecies, it is in the Catholic Church alone you will find them. In the Catholic Church alone are you placed in divine communication with the Blessed Spirits, nay with the Divine Spirit Himself. The Catholic Church alone is the realization of the true brotherhood of man; her precept of morality Divine charity, and her reward peace of mind and eternal happiness.

PART SECOND

I. Daily Acts

1. Morning Prayers

"I adore Thee at the dawning of the light."
"I will meditate on Thee in the morning."

Never, under any circumstances, miss your morning devotions. Offer up some prayer, however short before beginning your daily work. How can you otherwise expect God's blessing upon the day's toils and labors? how expect special strength in the hour of trial and temptation? how perform your duties aright? how avoid sin?

Rise betimes, and promptly, and at a regularly fixed hour. Excessive sleep is hurtful to soul and body.

Let your first thought be consecrated to God. Let your first look be upon the Crucifix or some other sacred object.

Dress quickly and modestly.

Then say your morning prayers. The following exercise may be profitably used.

✠ In the name of the Father, and of the Son, and of the Holy Ghost. Amen.

Blessed be the Holy and Undivided Trinity, now, and forever. Amen.

51

Glory be to the Father Who made me.

Glory be to the Son Who redeemed me.

Glory be to the Holy Ghost Who sanctifies me.

O my God, I believe in Thee; do Thou strengthen my faith. All my hopes are in Thee; do Thou secure them; I love Thee with my whole heart; teach me to love Thee daily more and more.

I am very sorry for ever having offended Thee; do Thou increase my sorrow. Grant me Thy grace that this day I may not offend Thee in thought, word, deed, or omission.

I offer to Thee, O my God, all my thoughts, words, actions, sufferings, and prayers of this day, in union with all that Thy Divine Son offered to Thee while on earth, and still offers to Thee in the Blessed Sacrament of the Altar. This offering I make unto Thee by the Power of Thy Divine Spirit, the Sanctifier, and place before Thy heavenly Throne through the pure hands of Mary Immaculate. Grant me the grace so to keep this offering before my mind during this day, that I may serve Thee faithfully and do Thy most Holy will in all things.

May the most just and adorable will of God be praised and glorified, for evermore. Amen.

I intend gaining all the indulgences I can during this day.

I again renew my determination to fulfil all my duties, to keep my promises, and carry out my good resolutions, especially. . . . Help me to do so, O my God, by the assistance of Thy Divine grace.

O Sweet Spirit of God, be Thou my Helper and Protector, my Guide and my Comforter this day, and all the days of my life. Grant that I may heed Thy Divine inspirations and faithfully obey them. Enlighten me to know what is right, and give me strength to do it.

Sweet Mary, my Mother, Immaculate Spouse of the Holy Ghost, do thou assist me by thy powerful intercession. O thou, who art the Health of the weak, the Refuge of sinners, the Help of Christians, pray for me.

St. Joseph, our protector, pray for me.

My good Angel guardian, and you my dear Patron—pray for me.

All ye holy Angels and Saints of God, intercede for me.

May the Lord bless us, and preserve us from all evil, and bring us to life everlasting. Amen.

May the souls of the Faithful, through the mercy of God, rest in peace. Amen.

"Our Father"—"Hail Mary"—"I Believe."

2. During the Day

Before, and after meals, bless yourself and say your grace. God is the giver of all things.

Before any important undertaking, invoke the aid of the Holy Ghost, saying:

Come, Holy Spirit, take entire possession of my heart and soul. Enlighten and strengthen me by Thy grace, that I may do all things well. May I never have any other end in view but the greater honor and glory of God, the good of my soul and the welfare of my neighbor.

At work, do not lose sight of God altogether, but make use now and then of a little ejaculatory prayer, such as—

O Holy Spirit, deign to bless and sanctify the work of Thy servant.

My Jesus, have mercy! Mary, help!

All ye holy Angels and Saints of God, pray for me.

May God be known, praised, and loved by all men!

All for Thy Sacred Heart, O Jesus, through Mary.

O Sacred Heart of Jesus, I implore the grace to love Thee daily more and more.

Jesus, meek and humble of heart, make my heart like unto Thine.

In time of temptation, at once call upon God for help:

O God, come to my assistance! O Lord, make haste to help me.

Holy Mary, pray for me.

Sweet Spirit of God, depart not from me.

I hate and detest sin above every evil.

May I rather die than offend Thee, O my God.

Should you fall into sin, be not discouraged, but beg at once for pardon and forgiveness:

O my God, I am very sorry that I have offended Thee. By the help of Thy grace, I will not offend Thee any more.

O Eternal Father, I offer to Thee the sufferings and the death of Thy Divine Son to atone for my sins.

Before spiritual readings or hearing the word of God, say:

Divine Spirit of Truth, teach me to know Thee! Sweet Spirit of Love, urge me to love Thee!

Before study, ask for help:

Divine Spirit of Wisdom, enable me to acquire that knowledge which shall be profitable to me for time and for eternity.

May this study lead me to know Thee Who art the God of all knowledge and understanding. And may I come to know Thee only that I may be the better able to love Thee.

When any trouble or misfortune befalls you, do not murmur or complain. Remember the Holy Ghost is in a special manner the Paraclete, the Comforter; pray for strength and courage:

Sweet Spirit of heavenly consolation, give solace and peace to my poor soul in its present hour of trial.

O my Father, if it be possible, let this chalice pass from me. Yet, not my will, but Thine, be done!

Give me grace to carry my cross patiently, out of love for Thee, who hast suffered so much for me. O Jesus, may I live, suffer, and die in union with Thee. Amen.

On beholding your neighbor in suffering or distress, compassionate him for Jesus' sake. If you are able to help him, do so. Console him in his afflictions. A kind word is balm to an aching heart. If you cannot do more at least offer up a prayer in his behalf:

O Jesus who Thyself wert once poor, and didst suffer untold agonies, pity the poor and afflicted in their sorrow and miseries.

O Divine Paraclete, comfort Thou the needy and sorrowful.

On passing a Church, enter for a moment to adore Jesus in the Most Blessed Sacrament of the Eucharist.

O Sacrament most holy! O Sacrament divine!
All praise and thanksgiving be every moment thine!
Blessed be Jesus in the Most Holy Sacrament of the Altar!

Seeing a picture or statue of our Blessed Lady, say:

Blessed be the Holy and Immaculate Conception of the Blessed Virgin Mary.

3. Night Prayers

*"Evening and morning I will speak to
the Lord, and He shall hear my voice,"*

Never retire to rest without having first devoutly said your night prayers. As by prayer you began the day in the name of God, so also should you close the day and retire for the night by invoking His blessing upon you.

Place yourself in God's presence and say very attentively:

✠ In the name of the Father, and of the Son, and of the Holy Ghost. Amen.

Blessed be the Holy and undivided Trinity, now and forever more. Amen.

Glory be to the Father Who made me.

Glory be to the Son Who redeemed me.

Glory be to the Holy Ghost Who sanctifies me.

"Our Father"—"Hail Mary"—"I believe."

I confess to Almighty God, to blessed Mary, ever Virgin, to blessed Michael the Archangel, to blessed John the Baptist, to the holy Apostles Peter and Paul, and to all the Saints! that I have sinned exceedingly in thought, word, and deed, through my fault, through my fault, through my most grievous fault. Therefore I beseech blessed Mary ever Virgin, blessed Michael the Archangel, blessed John the Baptist, the Holy Apostles Peter and Paul, and all the Saints, to pray to the Lord our God for me.

I give Thee thanks, Almighty God, for all Thou hast

done for me this day and all the days of my life. I likewise return Thee thanks in the name of all Thy creatures for all the blessings Thou hast ever bestowed upon
them.

Divine Spirit, searcher of men's heart, enlighten my
mind that I may see wherein I have sinned this day, and
make me truly sorry for all the evil I have done.

Now pause for a few moments and examine how you have
spent the day. If you find you have acted amiss anyway, be
sincerely contrite, should you be conscious of grievous sin,
resolve to go to confession as soon as possible; and repent
again of all the sins of your whole life.

O my God, I am sorry for ever having offended Thee,
because Thou art so good in Thyself, and art so good to
me, and with the help of thy grace, I will never offend
Thee again.

O Eternal Father, I offer to Thee the most Precious
Blood of Jesus in satisfaction for my sins, and the sins,
likewise, of the whole world.

Mary, Refuge of sinners, pray for me!

May the Blessed Virgin Mary, St. Joseph, and all the
Angels and Saints pray for me, that I may be preserved
this night from sin and all evils. And do Thou, through
their intercession, grant me the grace of a happy death.
Amen.

May the Lord bless us and preserve us, and bring us
to life everlasting. Amen.

May the souls of the Faithful, through the mercy of God, rest in peace. Amen.

Then modestly prepare and compose yourself to sleep. Let your last look be upon the crucifix or some other pious emblem, and let your mind be employed in dwelling upon some holy thought. Make use also of some ejaculatory prayer:

Into thy hands, O Lord, I commend my Spirit. Lord Jesus, receive my soul.

Jesus, Mary, Joseph; I offer you my heart and my soul.

Jesus, Mary, Joseph; assist me in my last agony.

Jesus, Mary, Joseph; may I breathe forth my last sigh in peace with you. Amen.

II. The Holy Sacrifice of the Mass

1. Mass the Sacrifice of the New Law

Holy Mass is the Sacrifice of the true Body and Blood of Jesus Christ, really present upon the Altar, under the appearances of bread and wine, and offered to God by the priest for the living and the dead.

Holy Mass is the same Sacrifice as that which was offered up by our Lord Himself on the Cross of Calvary, the manner alone of the offering being different. On the Cross, He actually died by the spilling of His Blood. On the Altar, He renews His Death in a mystical manner, without the real shedding of blood. This is done at the Consecration, for by the separate and distinct consecration of the two species, namely of the bread and of the wine, the blood of Christ is exhibited as being, once more, separate from His Body; and thus Jesus Christ is placed on the Altar, and offered to heaven, under the appearance of Death, as if slain again and immolated.

2. The four great ends of Mass

Holy Mass is offered to God for four great ends, corresponding to the four great duties we owe to Him. These are:

1. To praise, honor and adore the Infinite Majesty of God, Who is infinitely deserving of all the glory that can be given Him by His creatures.

2. To satisfy the Infinite Justice of God who is infinitely offended by the sins committed against Him.

3. To thank the Infinite Liberality of God Who requires an infinite return for all the favors bestowed upon His creatures.

4. To petition the Infinite Goodness of God Whom nothing but a pleading of infinite value can move to grant us all needful blessings.

When Jesus Christ by the Holy Ghost offered Himself unspotted to God on Mount Calvary, He paid infinite adoration to the Divine Majesty, gave infinite satisfaction to the Divine Justice, made an infinite return to the Divine Liberality and moved the Divine Goodness by an appeal of infinite efficacy.

Now in Holy Mass, Jesus places Himself entirely in your hands, that you may offer to God the same great sacrifice of infinite value for the same most excellent ends, in your behalf as well as for others, whether living or dead. For all who devoutly assist at Holy Mass, are made one with the priest, and along with him, present to heaven the Adorable Sacrifice. What would you, therefore, do without the Holy Mass? How could the world exist without these Sacred Mysteries?

"Holy Mass is the Sun of Christianity, the soul of Faith, the center of the Catholic Religion, the grand object of all her rites, ceremonies and sacraments; in a word, it is a summary of all that is grand and beautiful in the Church of God." (St. Leonard of Port-Maurice.)

"When a priest celebrates Holy Mass, he honors God, he rejoices the Angels, he edifies the Church he helps the living, he obtains rest for the departed, and makes himself partaker of all things." (*Following of Christ.*)

With the view, therefore, that God may receive from His creatures that clean oblation which alone is worthy of Him, and that the Faithful be not deprived of the immense benefit of the same adorable sacrifice, Holy Church commands her children under pain of grievous sin, to hear Mass on all Sundays and Holidays of obligation. But, surely, no Catholic who has any right idea of the importance and value of Holy Mass, will remain satisfied with this. He will attend Holy Mass as often as he can on week days as well. He will, likewise, have Masses offered up by the priest, both for himself and others, living or dead.

3. A Devout Method of Hearing Mass

At the beginning of Mass, recollect yourself, briefly examine your conscience, and make a fervent act of contrition;

then implore the aid of the Divine Spirit to enable you to hear Mass devoutly and profitably, and make the following general act of offering:

Eternal Father, I offer Thee the sacrifice which Thy Beloved Son Jesus made of Himself on the Cross, and now renews on the altar. I offer it in the name of all creatures together with all the Masses which have been said, and will be said, throughout the whole world: to adore Thee and to give Thee the honor due to Thee; to render Thee befitting thanks for Thy numberless benefits; to appease Thy anger, and to satisfy for our many sins; to supplicate Thy mercy for myself, for the Church, for the whole world, and for the Holy souls in Purgatory,

Now divide the Mass into four parts: according to its four great ends.

In the first part—from the beginning to the Gospel—place yourself in the presence of God, and at the thought of His Infinite Majesty acknowledge your utter dependence upon Him; and with sentiments of deep humiliation, arising from a feeling conviction of your nothingness and sinfulness, say to Him:

O my God! I adore Thee. I acknowledge Thee to be the Lord and Master of my whole being. All that I am, and all that I have, is from Thee. Without Thee, I am nothing. Without Thee, I can do nothing.

O Divine Majesty! I wish to adore Thee as the Angels

and Blessed do now in heaven. But since I am only a poor worthless creature, utterly unable to lay at Thy feet the tribute of adoration which Thy Sovereign Majesty deserves, I offer to Thee in the power of Thy Divine Spirit, the homage of infinite praise and glory which my Jesus now renders to Thee on Thy altar.

Come, O my soul, let us adore, and fall down. Let us weep before the Lord that made us. For He is the Lord our God, and we are His people and the sheep of His pasture.

To Thee be given benediction, and honor, and glory, and power for ever and ever.

Glory be to the Father! Glory be to the Son! Glory be to the Holy Ghost; now, and for ever more. Amen!

Close the Book—and reflect for a moment. By hearing Mass devoutly, even we who are dust and ashes, can offer to God an act of adoration truly infinite. Filled with this thought, cease not making a humble and sincere protestation from the depth of your heart, of your ardent desire to pay to God this infinite homage of worship due to Him.

In the second part of the Mass—from the Gospel to the Elevation—fulfill the second duty you owe to God, that, namely, of satisfying His Divine Justice outraged by sin.

Look back upon your past life; consider the many and grievous sins you have perhaps committed; acknowledge the fearful debt you have contracted towards the Divine Justice, and then say with feelings of deep sorrow and regret:

O Father, I have sinned against heaven and before Thee. Pierced with bitter grief of soul I now utterly abhor and detest all my sins. Yet what can I offer Thee to fully make amends to Thy Divine Justice, which demands an infinite atonement? But behold! my Jesus once more offers Himself on Thy altar to pay the debt I cannot myself discharge. And, in the Power of Thy Divine Spirit, I present to Thee the infinite satisfaction which Thy Divine Son again makes to Thee for my sins and those of the whole world. I unite my voice with that of His most Precious Blood which cries to Thee for mercy.

Have mercy on me, O God, according to Thy great mercy, and according to Thy tender mercies, blot out my iniquity.

Turn away Thy face from my sins; and wash me yet more from my iniquity.

Create in me a clean heart, O God; and renew a right spirit within me.

Cast me not away from Thy face; and take not Thy Holy Spirit from me.

In Thee, O Lord, have I hoped. Oh! let me not be confounded.

Close the Book; and continue to make fervent acts of contrition and repentance in the language that your heart may inspire. Mark well your worst short coming—the sin into which you fall most frequently, and at once take the necessary steps to curb that predominant passion or unruly inclination which is the chief source of all true evil into which you are betrayed. Should you be in grievous sin, resolve to approach the tribunal of Penance at the earliest opportunity.

In the third part of the Mass—from the Elevation to the Communion—recall to mind the countless blessings God has bestowed upon you, and, in return, offer to Him the Precious Body and Blood of Jesus Christ, His well-beloved Son.

O my God! When I think of all the favors which Thou hast lavished upon me until this present moment, and which Thou art still disposed to pour out upon me, in time and in eternity, I feel overwhelmed with the weight of Thy bounty. Thou hast created me for everlasting happiness with Thee in heaven. Thou hast given me the grace to believe in Thee and in all Thy Church teaches. Thou hast placed at my disposal all the means necessary for my eternal salvation. Thou hast instituted the Holy Sacraments, and especially the Most Blessed Sacrament of the Altar, to feed and nourish my soul. Thou hast given me Thy Divine Spirit to abide with me, to enlighten me, to strengthen me, to comfort me, to guide me through this valley of tears until I reach my one true home above. Oh! what return can I make to Thy infinite Liberality for all these mercies and blessings! Deign to look upon the Altar, and behold the priceless oblation which my Jesus makes of Himself to return Thee adequate thanks for all the gifts Thou hast extended to me and all mankind. This same sacrifice of infinite value and this most Holy Eucharist, I now offer to Thee, in the Power of the Holy Spirit. I offer it to thee in my own name and in that of all men. And I call upon all Thy creatures to praise Thy Sovereign Goodness. Then bless the Lord, O my soul; and let all that is within me, bless His Holy Name.

Close the Book, and continue to make similar acts of heartfelt gratitude in all simplicity and sincerity. God will be more pleased with these plain spontaneous expressions of gratefulness than if you were to speak your sentiments to Him in borrowed words, however choice and select.

In the fourth part—from the Communion to the end of the Mass—ask God for fresh blessings, both for yourself and others, through the same infinite Sacrifice of the Body and Blood of His Divine Son. Yet first make a spiritual communion, while the priest communicates sacramentally.

Sweet Jesus, my Lord, and my God: I firmly believe that Thou art truly present upon the Altar, under the lowly forms of bread and wine, to give Thyself as food for the spiritual refreshment of our souls. I am not worthy, that Thou shouldst enter into my heart; yet, only say the word, and my soul shall be healed.

O Divine Spirit, cleanse and purify my soul, to make it a fit dwelling place for my Lord and Savior. Since I cannot receive Thee now actually in Holy Communion, I beg of Thee to communicate Thyself to me spiritually. Come, sweet Jesus, come. I adore Thee. I love Thee. I return thanks to Thee.

Close your eyes, and reverently think of Jesus, present in your soul spiritually as though you had really received Him in Holy Communion. Adore, love, and thank Him. And then turning to your Heavenly Father, with childlike confidence and simplicity humbly ask Him in the name of Jesus, and in the Power of the Divine Spirit, for all needful blessings, for yourself and for others, living or dead.

O my God, I know I am not worthy of Thy mercies. I sincerely confess my utter unworthiness to receive anything from Thee. I do not deserve to be heard by Thee, on account of my sins, and because of my past ingratitude. Yet Thou canst not reject the prayer which Thy Divine Son addresses to Thee from this Altar, where He offers to Thee, on my behalf, His very Life and His Death.

O Eternal Father, in the sweet name of Jesus, I beg of Thee to give me Thy good Spirit, that henceforth I may at all times be wholly guided by Him, and may direct. all my ways according to Thy greater honor and glory, the good of my soul and the welfare of my neighbor.

And do Thou, O my Jesus, Son of the living God, by Thy most Precious Blood, cleanse me from all iniquities; and deliver me from all evils, past, present, and to come.

And Thou, O most Holy and Adorable Spirit, God the Holy Ghost, do Thou, by the Might of Thy Power, deign to impart to my weak will such strength as to be ever faithful to Thy commands, precepts, and inspirations; and never do Thou suffer me to be separated from Thee, Who, with the Father and the Son, liveth and reigneth, one God, world without end. Amen.

Close the Book; and continue praying for the objects and intentions uppermost in your mind: ask pardon for your sins; grace to overcome a temptation, to root out an evil habit, to practice some particular virtue, to obtain some special favor, spiritual or temporal; above all implore the grace of final perseverance. In like manner, pray for all men, especially the Sovereign Pontiff, bishops and priests and all religious; pray for your relations, benefactors, friends, and enemies; pray for the conversion of sinners and unbelievers; pray for the poor suffering souls in Purgatory. Pray, pray. Do not lose one moment of this most precious time. For you are not praying in your own name. You are now truly praying in the name of Jesus; nay, Jesus is now praying for you and with you. Whatsoever you now ask for, it will assuredly be given to you.

When the Mass is over, make a short thanksgiving for having been allowed to be present at this most Adorable Sacrifice and to share in its infinite merits. Then leave the Church, more firmly resolved than ever, on loving God and doing His

Holy Will. Quit the House of God, with the same disposition with which Mary, the mother of Jesus, St. John, the
beloved Disciple and the holy women, descended Calvary's
Hill after the Crucifixion. Strive to hear Mass after this manner as often as you can. Then will you please God on earth,
and lay up for yourself and others, endurable treasures in
heaven.

III. CONFESSION

1. The Power of the Sacrament of Penance

*"He that hideth his sins, shall not
prosper; but he that shall confess them,
shall obtain mercy."*

Jesus Christ gave to His Apostles, and to their lawful
successors, the bishops and priests of the Catholic Church,
power and authority to forgive the sins of all who heartily
repent of them and humbly acknowledge them in confession.

"Whose sins you shall forgive, they are forgiven them."
Should you be in the unhappy state of grievous sin, this Sacrament is all-important.

Consider the effects of mortal sin. It kills the soul, by
depriving it of sanctifying grace, which is its life. It stamps
and seals it with the mark of reprobation. It strips it of all past
merit, and robs it of all supernatural strength and energy. It
debars it from heaven, and condemns it to hell.

But when the repentant sinner worthily approaches the

Sacrament of Penance or Confession, his sins are at once blotted out; the eternal punishment due to them is cancelled; sanctifying grace is restored, and a new life imparted to him; the merits of all former good works is given back, and a special strength is conveyed to him to guard against sin in the future.

Confession, however, is beneficial, not only to souls in mortal sin, but to others besides. At all times, it cleanses the soul of past offenses, and also strengthens it against future relapses. Not only does it remit the eternal punishment, but it also lessens, and sometimes even entirely remits, according to the disposition of the penitent, the temporal penalties still due, not only for mortal but also for venial sin. It moreover fills the soul with a sweet tranquility and peace—of more real value than all the goods and pleasures of the world—arising as it does from the firm assurance that its sins are blotted out of the book of the recording angel.

"Go in peace; thy sins are forgiven thee."

Then be not content with going to Confession once a year, as the Church commands, under pain of mortal sin, but approach the Sacrament more frequently.

It is a dangerous thing to defer making one's peace with God.

2. Method of Confession

1. Ask for grace to make a good Confession

✠ In the name of the Father, and of the Son, and of the Holy Ghost. Amen.

Come, O Holy Spirit, and in Thine Infinite Mercy, enlighten my mind, and strengthen my will, that I may clearly see wherein I have offended Thine Infinite Majesty, and may be enabled to detect my sins, humbly confess them, and sincerely amend my life. Amen.

O Sweet Mary, my Mother, Immaculate Spouse of the Holy Ghost, Refuge of Sinners; assist me, by Thy intercession.

All ye holy Angels and Saints of God, pray for me. Amen.

"Our Father"—"Hail Mary"—"Glory be to the Father."

2. Carefully examine your conscience

Recollect yourself, and endeavor to find out the sins committed since your last confession. To this end, think over the ten commandments of God, the six precepts of the Church, and the particular duties of your special calling in life. Ask yourself in what points you have offended; try to remember the number of your sins, together with the circumstances, which may change their nature or add to their guilt. Be sincere and exact. It is not a pleasant task to search into one's own depravity; yet it has to be done.

3. Make a good act of contrition

Contrition is actual sorrow for all past sins with a firm determination to sin no more. It is absolutely essential to the Sacrament of Penance. Without true contrition, the Sacrament is invalid, even though the words of absolution should be pronounced. Endeavor, therefore, to excite in your heart a real sorrow for all the wrong you have done, together with a firm resolve to avoid in future, not only sin itself, but also everything leading to sin. To this end, think of God, Who, for His own sake, is infinitely deserving of all your love, and Whom you have wilfully offended by sin. Look upon your divine Savior, bleeding on the Cross; by sin you have crucified Him again in your heart. Ascend in spirit into heaven; sin has closed its gates against you. Descend in spirit into hell; sin has opened its gates to receive you. Dwell upon these thoughts for a little while. Then slowly recite an act of contrition.

O my God! I am heartily sorry that I have offended Thee by my sins. Do pardon and forgive me! I am determined, by the help of Thy grace, never to offend Thee again.

Lord, be merciful to me, a sinner.

Wash me yet more, O God, from my sins in the Most Precious Blood of Jesus, my dear Redeemer.

Jesus, mercy! Mary, help!

While waiting for your turn to enter the Confessional, employ the time in repeating acts of love and sorrow. Make use of the inspired words of the royal Penitent:

O Lord, rebuke me not in Thine anger, nor chastise me in Thy wrath.

Have mercy on me, O Lord, for I am weak; heal me, O Lord, for I am troubled.

Turn Thee, O Lord, and deliver my soul; O save me for Thy mercy's sake.

Rebuke me not, O Lord, in Thine indignation; neither chasten me in Thy sore displeasure.

For Thine arrows are fastened in me, and Thy hand presseth heavily upon me.

There is no health in my flesh, because of Thy wrath; there is no rest for my bones, because of my sins.

Mine iniquities are gone over my head, and as a heavy burden are become heavy upon me.

Lord, all my desire is before Thee, and my groaning is not hid from Thee.

I will declare mine iniquity, and I will be thoughtful of my sin.

Forsake me not, O Lord, my God; do not Thou depart from me.

Give heed unto my help, O Lord, Thou God of my salvation.

Have mercy upon me, O God, according to Thy great mercy. And according to the multitude of Thy tender mercies, blot out mine iniquity.

Wash me yet more from mine iniquity, and cleanse me from my sin.

I acknowledge mine iniquity, and my sin is always before me.

Thou shalt sprinkle me with hyssop, and I shall be cleansed.

Thou shalt wash me, and I shall be made whiter than snow.

Turn away Thy face from my sins; and blot out all mine iniquities.

Create in me a clean heart, O God, and renew a right spirit within me.

Cast me not away from Thy face, and take not Thy Holy Spirit from me.

Restore unto me the joy of Thy salvation and strengthen me with a perfect spirit.

A sacrifice unto God is a troubled spirit; a contrite and humble heart, O Lord, Thou wilt not despise.

Hear my prayer, O Lord, and let my cry come unto Thee.

Turn not away Thy face from me; in the day when I am in trouble, incline Thine ear unto me.

Oh! let Thine ears consider well the voice of my supplication.

If Thou, O Lord, wilt mark iniquities. Lord, who shall abide it?

With Thee there is merciful forgiveness; with Thee there is plenteous redemption.

Hear my prayer, O Lord; give ear to my supplication in Thy truth; hearken unto me for Thy justice sake.

Enter not into judgment with Thy servant; for in Thy sight shall no man living be justified.

I stretch forth my hands unto Thee; my soul gaspeth unto Thee, as earth without water.

Hear me speedily, O Lord; my spirit hath fainted away.

Make me to know the way wherein I should walk; for to Thee have I lifted up my soul.

Deliver me from mine enemies, O Lord, unto Thee have I fled; teach me to do Thy will, for Thou art my God.

Thy good Spirit shall lead me into the right land; for Thy name's sake, O Lord; Thou shalt quicken me in Thy justice.

Thou shalt bring my soul out of trouble and, in Thy mercy, Thou shalt destroy mine enemies.

Thou shalt destroy all them that afflict my soul, for I am Thy servant.

4. Humbly confess your sins

Kneeling down make the sign of the Cross, and say:

Pray, Father, give me your blessing, for I have sinned. Since my last Confession which was. . . . I accuse myself of the following sins.

Now tell your sins in all sincerity and humility. Remember, you now kneel at the feet of one who holds the place of Jesus. Never excuse yourself. Speak of your own sins only. Should you feel any difficulty, ask the Confessor for help.

Having confessed all the sins you remember, say:

For these, and for all other sins, which I cannot at present call to my remembrance, I am heartily sorry, purpose amendment for the future, and most humbly ask pardon of God, and absolution of you, my Ghostly Father.

Then give attentive ear to the instructions and advice of your Confessor. God speaks through him to you. Humbly accept the penance enjoined by him.

While the priest pronounces the words of absolution, bow down your head, and, with great humility, ask God once more to have mercy on you, and repeat, with great sorrow, the following or similar, act of contrition:

O my God, I am very sorry for ever having offended Thee, because Thou art so good, and, with the help of Thy holy grace, I will not sin again. Amen.

5. Faithfully perform the penance enjoined in confession

Do not delay performing your penance. If the confessor has not pointed out any particular time when the penance should be performed, complete the Sacrament at once by saying your penance then and there. If a special time has been pointed out, be careful to attend to it as directed.

6. Return sincere thanks to God

Before leaving the Church, do not fail to return sincere thanks to God from the depth of your heart, for having, in His mercy, bestowed upon you, once more, peace and pardon.

Remember how our Lord complained of the ungrateful lepers, whom He had healed: were not ten made clean, and where are the nine? Say, therefore, with a grateful heart:

O most loving and tender Father! How can I ever sufficiently thank Thee for all Thou hast done for me. By sin, I had abandoned Thee and turned away from Thee. Thou couldst have cut me off in the midst of my sins. Yet Thou hast spared me. Thou didst most lovingly invite me to return to Thee, most kindly receive me, and most mercifully pardon me through the merits of Jesus, my Savior, and the operation of the Holy Ghost. For these, and all other favors, I thank Thee most sincerely from the bottom of my heart. I call upon all creatures to join me in praising and blessing Thine infinite mercy and goodness. Ah! grant that I may never be so ungrateful as to again abandon Thee by sin. Rather will I die, than ever more offend Thee.

O Divine Spirit, penetrate my soul with true horror and loathing of sin. Grant that I may begin, from this very moment, to be more exact in the fulfillment of all my duties, to avoid sin and all its dangerous occasions, and should temptations again assail me, I rely upon Thy help and assistance.

I again renew my good resolutions, especially. . . . I am determined to avoid this particular sin. . . . to shun such or such an occasion of sin. . . . to break off such or such an evil habit. . . . Grant me Thy grace to do so.

O Mary, my Mother, Spouse of the Holy Ghost, Strength of the weak, Refuge of sinners, assist me by Thy prompt intercession.

All ye holy Angels and Saints of God, pray for me.

"Our Father," "Hail Mary," "Glory be to the Father"—for the grace of final perseverance.

Conclude with the following verses from the Psalms:

Blessed are they whose iniquities are forgiven, and whose sins are covered.

Blessed is the man to whom the Lord hath not imputed sin, and in whose spirit there is no guile.

I have acknowledged my sin unto Thee, and mine iniquity I have not concealed.

I said, I will confess against myself mine iniquity with the Lord, and Thou hast forgiven the wickedness of my sin.

Thou art my refuge from the trouble which hath encompassed me; my joy. Deliver me from them that surround me.

Bless the Lord, O my soul, and let all that is within me, bless His holy name. Bless the Lord, O my soul, and never forget all He hath done for thee.

Who forgiveth all thy iniquities; Who healeth all thy diseases.

Who redeemeth thy life from destruction; Who crowneth thee with mercy and compassion.

The Lord is compassionate and merciful; long suffering and plenteous in mercy.

He will not always be angry; nor will He threaten for ever.

He hath not dealt with us according to our sins; nor rewarded us according to our iniquities.

As far as the east is from the west, so far hath He removed our iniquities from us.

As a father hath compassion on his children, so hath the Lord compassion on them that fear Him.

For He knoweth our frame; He remembereth that we are dust.

Bless the Lord, all ye His Angels; bless the Lord all ye His hosts.

Bless the Lord all His works; in every place of His dominion, O my soul, bless thou the Lord.

IV. Holy Communion

1. The Last will of Jesus

"Amen, amen, I say unto you: Except you eat the flesh of the Son of Man and drink His Blood, you shall not have life in you."

Jesus, before leaving this world, made His last will and testament. And what was it He bequeathed unto you? Oh! the infinite depth of the love of Jesus for man! He gave you Himself! And for what purpose? To be the very food of your soul. "Take and eat. This is my body. Take and drink. This is my Blood. My Flesh is meat, indeed. My Blood is drink, indeed."

Can you resist? Will you refuse? Why then are you so backward in approaching this heavenly Banquet? Why are you so cold and indifferent in regard to this most Divine Sacrament? Surely, if you but realized Who it is that invites you, your heart would be all on fire with love for Him. Then shake off that sloth and indifference. Rouse your fervor. Receive Holy Communion often, and at regular intervals, and do so with the utmost fervor and devotion of your soul. Thus shall you be made all one with Jesus. His Life will impress itself upon you. You shall grow in grace and virtue. Your evil inclinations will be checked. A pledge of life everlasting will be given to you, and your body will be fitted for a glorious resurrection.

2. Preparation for Holy Communion

The effects of Holy Communion are simply boundless! Yet your share in them will be in proportion to your preparation. If you enlarge your heart by a devout and fervent preparation, your soul will be filled with an abundance of Divine blessings both for yourself and others.

The following prayers will assist you to make a good preparation. Yet do not confine yourself to them. Speak rather to God in your own words.

Ask for help:—O my God, since without Thee I can do nothing, do Thou, by the power of Thy Divine grace, enable me to make a good and a worthy Communion.

Let Thy Holy Spirit so cleanse my soul and purify the affections of my heart, that Jesus Christ, Thy Divine Son, may be pleased to enter and abide therein. Amen.

O Mary, Mother of Jesus, help me.

All ye Holy Angels and Saints of God, pray for me. Amen.

Make your intention:—O Jesus, my God, I wish to receive Thee in remembrance of Thy most bitter Passion and Death on the Cross—to thank Thee for all favors and blessings bestowed upon me and upon all mankind—to acquire and practice the virtues necessary for my state in life—to obtain special strength to fulfill faithfully the commandments of God, the precepts of the Church, and my particular duties—to pray for the Sovereign Pontiff, the bishops and priests of the Catholic Church, all religious, both men and women, for my relatives, benefactors, friends and enemies, for the conversion of sinners and unbelievers, and lastly for the relief of the suffering souls in Purgatory.

In a special manner do I intend to offer up this Holy Communion to obtain . . . or on behalf of . . .

Grant, O God, that as I offer this Communion to the honor of Thy Name, for the good of my own poor soul, and the welfare of my neighbor it may be to me a means of obtaining an increase of Thy Divine grace, here on earth, and an increase of glory hereafter in heaven. Amen.

An Act of Faith:—O Jesus, my Hidden God, because Thou hast the words of eternal life, and because Thou hast said it, I believe that Thou are really and truly present in the Holy Sacrament of the Altar, and that I shall receive in the Holy Communion Thine own true Body and Blood, for the food and nourishment of my poor soul.

Lord Jesus, this I firmly believe, with all my heart and soul. Do Thou strengthen my faith. Amen.

An Act of Adoration:—O Jesus, Thou art my God and my Redeemer. I humbly bow down and prostrate myself before Thee, Who art really and truly present in this most Holy Sacrament.

I acknowledge that all I am, have, or will have, comes from Thee, so that I am entirely depending upon Thee for everything.

I adore Thee in union with Thy Angels and Saints. Thou art my Lord, Thou art my God, my first Beginning and my last End.

An Act of Humility:—Jesus, my God, when I consider my many and grievous sins, by which I have offended Thy infinite Majesty, I confess that I am utterly unworthy even to approach Thee, much less to receive Thee into my sinful soul. Who art Thou, and what am I? Thou art Almighty, and I am weak and helpless. Thou art infinitely rich in every Perfection, and I am poor and lowly. Thou art All-holy, and I am a wretched sinner. Lord, I am not worthy that Thou shouldst enter under my roof; say but the word, and my soul shall be healed.

An Act of Sorrow:—O Jesus, my God, I once more loathe and detest, from my inmost soul, all the sins and failings by which I have so often and so grievously outraged Thy Divine Goodness and Majesty. Henceforth I am fully determined to sin no more. Do Thou help me by Thy holy grace.

O Lord, be merciful to me, a poor sinner, Penetrate my soul with a lasting sorrow for my sins—with such a sorrow as shall enable me to put away whatever is displeasing to Thee. Amen.

An Act of Love and Desire:—O Jesus, my God, I love Thee with all my heart and soul, above all things; at least, I most earnestly desire to love thee as I ought. May, henceforth, all my thoughts, words, and actions prove to Thee that I truly love Thee. And because I love Thee, O my Jesus, I now most sincerely desire to receive Thee into my poor soul, in spite of all my unworthiness.

Oh, that I had the love of Thy Blessed Mother, and of all the Angels and Saints, wherewith to receive Thee!

An Invocation of the Holy Ghost:—O Divine Spirit of Love, do Thou fill my soul with the fire of Thy Divine Love to cleanse it yet more from every stain, and clothe it with grace and beauty, so that Jesus may be pleased to come and enter therein. O Thou Who, by Thy grace, didst overshadow Mary to make her the worthy Mother of the Son of God, so overshadow now my poor soul by the might of Thy Divine grace, that it may become a worthy dwelling-place for Jesus, the Spouse of my soul.

Then do Thou accompany me, O Divine Guide, to that heavenly Banquet, wherein Christ is made my food, where the memory of His Passion is renewed, where my soul is filled with grace, and where there is given unto me a pledge of everlasting life.

Yes, may I receive Thee, Dear Jesus, in the Power and the Love of Thy Holy Spirit, for Thy greater honor and glory, the good of my soul, and the welfare of my neighbor.

Come to me, sweetest Jesus. Come to me and take entire possession of my whole being, so that I may be wholly thine, and Thou wholly mine, in time and in eternity. Amen.

These acts, slowly and devoutly recited, will dispose your soul for a worthy reception of the Most Blessed Sacrament.

If you have to wait awhile repeat these acts, not so much in the words here given, as in words prompted by the feelings of your own heart. The following verses from Sacred Scripture will aid you still more to acquire the true disposition of mind and heart. Read them slowly and seriously reflect upon their meaning:

Wisdom hath built herself a house; she hath mingled her wine and set forth her table.

Come eat my bread, and drink the wine which I have mingled for you.

Why do you spend money for that which is not bread, and your labor for that which doth not satisfy you?

You that have no money, make haste, and eat. Come ye, buy wine and milk without money, and without price.

Labor not for the meat which perisheth, but for that which endureth unto life everlasting, which the Son of Man will give you.

I am the Bread of Life.

Your fathers did eat manna in the desert and are dead.

I am the living Bread which came down from heaven.

If any man eat of this Bread, he shall live for ever.

And the Bread that I will give, is My Flesh for the life of the world.

Amen, amen, I say unto you: Except you eat the Flesh of the Son of Man and drink His Blood, you shall not have life in you.

He that eateth My Flesh, and drinketh My Blood, hath everlasting life; and I will raise him up on the last day.

For My Flesh is meat indeed, and My Blood is drink indeed.

He that eateth My Flesh, and drinketh My Blood abideth in Me, and I in him.

As the living Father hath sent Me, and I live by the

Father, so he that eateth Me, the same also shall live by Me.

Take ye and eat. This is My Body. Drink ye all of this, for this is my Blood.

I am with you all days, even to the consummation of the world.

Come to Me all ye that labor and are burdened, and I will refresh you. I will give peace to your souls.

As often as you shall eat this bread, and drink the chalice, you shall show the Death of the Lord until He come.

Whosoever shall eat this bread, or drink the chalice of the Lord unworthily, shall be guilty of the Body and the Blood of the Lord.

Let a man prove himself, and so let him eat of that bread and drink of the chalice.

He that eateth and drinketh unworthily eateth and drinketh judgment to himself, not discerning the Body of the Lord.

There is not any other nation so great, that hath gods so nigh them, as our God is present to us.

I will praise Thee, O Lord my God, with my whole heart, and I will glorify Thy name for ever.

Thou didst feed Thy people with the food of angels, and gavest them bread from heaven, having in it all that is delicious, and the sweetness of every taste.

He hath not done in like manner to every nation,

and His judgments He hath not made manifest to them.

Blessed be the name of the Lord, from henceforth and for ever more.

I will go into the Altar of God; to God Who giveth joy to my youth.

Why art thou sad, O my soul, and why dost thou disquiet me?

I will go over into the palace of the wonderful tabernacle even to the House of God.

How lovely are Thy Tabernacles, O Lord of Hosts!

My soul longeth and fainteth for the Courts of the Lord.

As the hart panteth after the fountains of water so my soul panteth after Thee, O God.

Come, Lord Jesus! Amen.

When the time arrives for you to receive Holy Communion, approach the Altar rail with folded hands and downcast eyes. Renew your acts of love and sorrow, and when the priest turns towards the people, holding the Sacred Host in his hand, strike your breast, and say:

Lord, I am not worthy that Thou shouldst enter under my roof; say but the word, and my soul shall be healed.

When about to receive, hold the Communion-cloth under your chin, close your eyes, and with your mouth moderately open and your tongue resting on the lower lip, receive the

Sacred Particle with all humility and devotion, and swallow it at once. Then modestly retire to your place, kneel and let your feelings of wonder and astonishment, of love and reverence, yield to expressions arising from your own heart. The following prayers are meant only as a help. Do not confine yourself to them. If you do use them, say them slowly, pausing from time to time to reflect on their meaning.

Listen, as it were, to Jesus speaking to you within your own heart, encouraging you, comforting you, urging you on to good.

Do not leave Church at once. You should devote at least ten or fifteen minutes in returning due thanks to our Lord. Make the best of your time. These are most precious moments. Jesus remains with you under the Sacramental species only for a short time. Say to Him, as Jacob said to the Angel: "I will not let Thee go, except Thou bless me." If the infallible Truth has assured you, that whatsoever you ask the Father in His name, will be given unto you, what blessing is there that your heavenly Guest will not bestow upon you, and upon others, when you pray to Him after receiving Holy Communion? For if ever you pray in the name of Jesus, you most certainly do so now when He personally reposes in your heart and soul.

3. Thanksgiving after Holy Communion

An Act of Faith:—O Jesus, my God and my Redeemer. Thy word is Truth. I firmly believe that this is Thy Sacred Body and Blood which I have just received, and that Thou art now really and truly present within me.

An Act of Adoration:—O Jesus, my God! I can only prostrate myself before Thee, and cry out from the depths of my heart: Thou art my Lord and my God, my God and my All!

An Act of Humility:—O Jesus, my God! Thou art infinite in all Perfections; and I am but dust, and unto dust shall I return. Depart from me, O Lord, for I am a sinful man. Yet, O my Sweet Jesus, if Thou leavest me, to whom shall I go? What will become of me? Rather will I say: Stay with me, Lord; abide always within my heart; and may my heart make every sacrifice for Thee.

An Act of Love:—O Jesus, my God, Infinite Love, Source and Fount of all that is true, of all that is good, of all that is beautiful, how can I help loving Thee, both because of Thine own Infinite Goodness and because of Thy Goodness and kindness to me! My Jesus! I love Thee with my whole heart. Oh! may I love Thee daily more and more! Amen.

An Act of Petition:—O Jesus, my God! Behold me, in all my poverty and weakness! Thou art rich; help me! Thou art mighty; strengthen me! Thou art Light, in which all knowledge is contained; enlighten my darkness!

I pray Thee especially. . . . (here mention your particular requests.)

Who hath ever trusted in Thee, O my sweet Jesus, and hath been confounded? Relying upon Thy Goodness and Thy promises, I trust that Thou will grant me forgiveness of all my sins and the grace of persevering until death in Thy Holy service. Amen.

Continue to pray for your own needs, and all the wants of Holy Church; for all bishops and priests; for religious men and women; for Christian Kings and Princes and all in authority; for your relations, benefactors, friends and enemies; for poor sinners and unbelievers, and for the poor suffering souls in Purgatory.

An Act of Thanksgiving:—O Jesus, my God! I thank Thee from the very bottom of my heart for having condescended to notice me and to visit me, Thy most unworthy creature.

Would that I could thank Thee even as the Blessed do in heaven!

O Mary, my Mother! By the love Thou hast for Jesus, Thy Divine Son, help me to thank Him.

All ye Holy Angels and Saints of God, unite with me in rendering due thanks to God for His tender mercies towards me.

An Invocation of the Holy Ghost after Holy Communion:—O Divine Spirit! Through Thee Jesus was given to the world. Through Thee, he has now been given to me, to nourish and strengthen my poor soul. Do Thou fully apply to my soul the wonderful effects of this most Divine Sacrament.

Do Thou give utterance to my heart in praising, loving and adoring my Jesus in the manner He deserves, or rather, do Thou Thyself, "who prayest for me with unspeakable groanings" praise, love and adore Him for me, and grant both to me and to all others the favors and blessings for which I have been asking.

Do Thou impart unto me a sincere lasting love and affection for Jesus in the most Holy Sacrament of the Altar.

Do Thou so strengthen my weak will, that I may keep all, my good resolutions, and persevere unto the end in Christ's holy service.

Do Thou so rule over me, that I may be able to resist all base inclinations and overcome my evil passions.

Do Thou so assist me by Thy Divine grace, that I may be ready to make every sacrifice, nay, to lay down life itself, to prove my love for Jesus my God and my Redeemer. Amen.

The following thoughts and affections are taken from the Psalms, and may profitably be used after Holy Communion:

O how great is the multitude of Thy sweetness, O Lord, which Thou hast wrought for them that hope in Thee.

O how hast Thou multiplied Thy mercy of God. The children of men shall put their trust under the covert of Thy wings.

They shall be inebriated with the plenty of Thy home; and Thou shalt make them drink of the torrent of Thy pleasure.

With Thee, there is the fountain of life, and in Thy light we shall see light.

God commanded the clouds from above, and opened the doors of heaven.

He rained down manna upon them and gave them the bread of heaven.

Men ate the bread of Angels. He sent them provision in plenty.

Who is man, that Thou art mindful of him? or the son of man, that Thou visitest him?

One thing I asked of the Lord. That I might see the Delight of the Lord and visit His temple.

Who will give me wings like a dove, and I will fly and be at rest?

I will be glad and rejoice, for Thou hast regarded my humility.

He hath hidden me in His tabernacle. He hath protected me in the secret places of His tabernacle.

I have loved, O Lord, the beauty of Thy house, and the place where Thy glory dwelleth.

I will love Thee, O Lord, my strength. O Lord, my helper and my Redeemer.

The Lord is my light and my salvation, whom shall I

fear? The Lord is the protector of my life, of whom shall I be afraid?

If armies in camp should stand together against me, my heart shall not fear. If a battle should rise up against me, in this will I be confident.

In Thee, O Lord, have I hoped; let me never be confounded.

I will sing to the Lord as long as I live; I will sing praise, O my God, while I have my being.

Bless the Lord, O my soul, and let all that is within me, bless His holy name.

Bless the Lord, O my soul, and never forget all He hath done for thee.

Save, O Lord, Thy people, and bless Thine inheritance, and rule them, and exalt them for ever.

Let Thy mercy be upon us, as we have hoped in Thee. Amen.

4. Indulgenced Prayer After Communion

Do not fail to endeavor to gain an indulgence after communion, i.e., a remission partial or total of the temporal penalties that may still be due to the Justice of God on account of your sins. The Sovereign Pontiffs have granted a Plenary Indulgence to all the faithful who, having confessed their sins, with contrition, and received Holy Communion, shall say the following prayers before an image or representation of Christ Crucified. Dispose your soul by making a fervent act of contrition. Then recite slowly and fervently;

Behold me, O good and sweetest Jesus, prostrate in thy presence, I pray Thee with the utmost fervor of my soul, and beseech Thee that Thou wouldst impress upon my heart lively sentiments of faith, hope and charity, true contrition for my sins, and a most firm purpose of amendment; whilst I contemplate, with all the affection of my soul, Thy Five Wounds and ponder them over in my mind, having before my eyes the words which, long ago, David the Prophet spoke in his own person concerning Thee, my Jesus: "They digged my hands and my feet, they numbered all my bones."

Recite five times "Our Father, Hail Mary and Glory" for the intentions of the Sovereign Pontiff.

5. Divine Praises

Blessed be God.
Blessed be His Holy Name.
Blessed be Jesus Christ, true God and true man.
Blessed be the Name of Jesus.
Blessed be His Most Sacred Heart.
Blessed be Jesus in the Most Holy Sacrament of the Altar.
Blessed be the great Mother of God, Mary most holy.
Blessed be her holy and Immaculate Conception.
Blessed be the Name of Mary, Virgin and Mother.
Blessed be God in His Angels and in His Saints.

6. Soul of Christ

Soul of Christ, sanctify me!
Body of Christ, save me!
Blood of Christ, inebriate me!
Water from the side of Christ, wash me!
Passion of Christ, strengthen me!
O Good Jesus, hear me!
Hide me within Thy wounds!
Suffer me not to be separated from Thee!
From the malicious enemy defend me!
In the hour of my death, call me!
And bid me come to Thee!
And with Thy Saints I may praise Thee!
For ever and ever! Amen.

During the day, occasionally think of Jesus, Whom in the morning you received into your heart and soul. Let the effects of Holy Communion show themselves in your conduct. Jesus rested on your tongue for a moment when you received Him. Then, let your speech be kind, prudent, modest. Jesus descended into your heart. Then allow Him to reign therein as on His throne and to rule over all your thoughts, desires and affections. Jesus sanctified your very body. Then take care to preserve it in all sobriety, modesty, and chastity. Jesus came to give you of His life. Then let Him truly live in you. Let His virtues be reproduced in you. Practice especially that spirit of self-denial and sacrifice, so necessary for every true Christian. Implore the aid of the Divine Spirit to enable you to do so.

PART THIRD

Special Exercises in Honor
of God the Holy Ghost

I. Daily Act of Consecration to the Holy Ghost

O God the Holy Ghost, Infinite Love of the Father and of the Son, through the pure hands of Mary, Thy Immaculate Spouse, I place myself, this day, and all the days of my life, upon Thy chosen Altar, the Divine Heart of Jesus, as a holocaust to Thee, O Thou Consuming Fire, being firmly resolved, now more than ever, to hear Thy voice, and do, in all things, Thy most Holy and Adorable Will.

Come, O Holy Ghost, fill the hearts of Thy faithful and kindle in them the fire of Thy Divine Love!

Protect us under the shadow of Thy wings!

Mayest Thou every where be known, praised, loved, and adored, in time and in eternity! Amen.

II. Prayer of St. Francis of Assisi for the gift of the Divine Spirit

O Almighty and Eternal God, most Just and Merciful, grant to us miserable creatures Thy grace, that we may always do what we know to be Thy will, and always will what Thou willest, that, thus purified and enlightened interiorly, and so inflamed with the fire of Thy Holy Spirit we may follow in the footsteps of Thy Beloved Son Jesus Christ, and thus arrive at the possession of Thee who livest and reignest, one God, world without end. Amen.

III. Divine Praises in honor of God the Holy Ghost

Blessed be God, the Father in Heaven!

Blessed be God the Son, Redeemer of the world!

Blessed be God the Holy Ghost, the Sanctifier!

Blessed be the Substantial Love of the Father and the Son!

Blessed be the Paraclete!

Blessed be the Teacher of all Truth!

Blessed be the Divine Spouse of Mary most holy!

Blessed be the Immaculate Spouse of the Holy Ghost, the Virgin Mother of our Lord and Savior, Jesus Christ!

IV. Prayer of the Servants of the Holy Ghost

On my knees before the great cloud of witnesses, I offer myself, soul and body, to Thee, eternal Spirit of God. I adore the brightness of Thy purity, the unerring keenness of Thy justice, and the might of Thy love.

Thou art the strength and light of my soul. In Thee I live and move and am. I desire never to grieve Thee by unfaithfulness to grace, and I pray with all my heart to be kept from the smallest sin against Thee. Make me faithful in every thought, and grant that I may always listen to Thy voice, watch for Thy light, and follow Thy gracious inspiration.

I cling to Thee, and give myself to Thee, and ask Thee, by Thy compassion, to watch over me in my weakness. Holding the pierced feet of Jesus, and looking at His five wounds, and trusting to His precious Blood, and adoring His open side and stricken heart, I implore Thee, adorable Spirit, Helper of my infirmity, so to keep me in Thy grace that I may never sin against Thee with the sin which Thou canst not forgive. Give me grace, O Holy Ghost, Spirit of the Father and the Son, to say to Thee, always and everywhere, "Speak, Lord; for Thy servant heareth."

V. Prayer of a soul in deep distress

O Divine Spirit of infinite Love! Divine Consoler, and of all comforters the best! To Thee I come in my present trouble and deep distress. Do Thou, in the all-powerful name of Jesus, my dear Redeemer, and out of love for Mary, His most afflicted Mother, and Thy Immaculate Spouse, come to my assistance, and comfort my poor sorrowful soul.

Lord, if it be possible, and pleasing to Thee, take this chalice of suffering from me. Yet not my will, but Thine, be done!

If it be Thy Holy Will that I should bear this cross, then give me Thy grace to accept it with all resignation, and carry it patiently out of love for Jesus, my Crucified Redeemer, and in atonement for my sins. And when the cross weighs heavily upon me, then, O sweet Spirit, uphold me by Thy Power and console me with Thy heavenly comfort.

"My soul hath fainted after Thy salvation: and in Thy word I have hoped exceedingly. My eyes have failed for Thy word, saying: When wilt Thou comfort me."

"The wicked have told me fables: but not as Thy law. All Thy statutes are truth. They have persecuted me unjustly: do Thou help me. They have almost made an end of me on earth: but I have not forsaken Thy commandments."

"I am Thine," O God of Love. By Thee have I been

justified and adopted. By Thee have I been signed and
sealed in the Blood of Jesus; by Thee am I guided and
directed. To Thee, therefore, I belong. Do Thou not
abandon me. "Incline unto mine aid, O God: O Lord,
make haste to help me."

"Save Thou me; for I am Thine."

VI. CANTICLE TO THE HOLY GHOST

I.

O Holy Ghost, my King, I worship Thee;
Creator of the world, I kneel to Thee;
O Light of uncreated Majesty,
O Love of God in threefold unity,
O Kiss of the Most Holy Trinity,
O Spouse of lily souls, I lean on Thee!
O gracious Paraclete, I worship Thee!

II.

O Holy Ghost, Thou most sweet Charity,
Thou sevenfold Ray of God's great majesty;
Thou sevenfold Glory of the Trinity;
Thou sevenfold Beauty of the Unity;
Thou sevenfold Gift from God's Eternity;
Breath of the uncreated One in Three,
O Holy Ghost, I praise and worship Thee!

III.

O Holy Ghost, Who givest life to me;
O Holy Ghost, Who givest strength to me;
O Holy Ghost, Who givest gifts to me;
Who willest all Thy gifts to give to me;
Who willest I should correspond with Thee;
O Holy Ghost, vouchsafe to live in me,
That this my heart may be a home for Thee.

IV.

Spirit of Wisdom, let me learn from Thee;
The falsehoods of the world to leave for Thee;
Spirit of Understanding, I would be
Enlightened with the fire that burns in Thee;
Spirit of Counsel, do Thou set me free
From tangled judgments that are not of Thee,
And guide me in the way of liberty.

V.

Spirit of Fortitude, O come to me,
In all my trials do Thou strengthen me;
Spirit of Heavenly Knowledge, give to me,
Thy grace divine to use this world for Thee,
And Thou, O Spirit Meek of Piety.
Make this my heart a home of peace to be,
A spring of overflowing charity.

VI.

Spirit of Holy Fear, O, I would be
Plunged in thy very depths, all steeped in Thee;
That sin may never more find place in me;
That imperfection may grow less in me;
That thought of self may pass away from me;
That God's eternal light may rest on me;
That I may live in Thee and Thou in me.

VII.

Great Ruler of the Church, I worship Thee;
The Giver of her gifts art Thou to me;
Her sacramental graces flow from Thee;
All power in earth and Heaven she draws from Thee;
Thou art her Breath, her Soul; she lives by Thee.
O Holy Ghost! O gift of God to me!
O Holy Ghost, with joy I worship Thee.

VII. Seven invocations to the Holy Ghost

1. Sweet Spirit of the Father and of the Son! Source of all life! Be Thou the Life of my soul; and may Thy sanctifying grace ever abide within me. Amen.

Our Father. Hail Mary. Glory be.

2. Fount of Infinite Goodness! Do Thou increase within me Faith, Hope, and Charity, so that I may

believe in Thy Word more firmly, rely on Thy Bounty more serenely, and love Thy Goodness more ardently. Amen.

Our Father. Hail Mary. Glory be.

3. Lord of Infinite Might and Power! Do Thou fortify my weakness and replenish me with Thy sevenfold spirit, so that I may ever be victorious over all my spiritual enemies and obtain the crown of Life. Amen.

Our Father. Hail Mary. Glory be.

4. Divine Spirit of Truth! Life and soul of Holy Church! Do Thou enable me to be always and everywhere a docile and obedient member of God's true Church, a loyal and devoted subject of the Sovereign Pontiff, Thy infallible mouth-piece on earth, and a zealous advocate of God's interests, by word and by example. Amen.

Our Father. Hail Mary. Glory be.

5. Divine Spirit of Sanctity! Source of infinite holiness! Do Thou take full possession of my whole being and do Thou sanctify me by enabling me to conform myself, on all occasions, and in all things, to Thy Most Holy and Adorable Will. Amen.

Our Father. Hail Mary. Glory be.

6. Divine Spirit of infinite Purity! Do Thou govern and direct all the movements and inclinations of my soul and body, that I may delight Thee by a pure, chaste and blameless life. Amen.

Our Father. Hail Mary. Glory be.

7. Divine Spirit of Love! Uncreated, Substantial Love of the Father and of the Son! Do Thou, Who art a consuming Fire, burn up within my sinful soul whatever is displeasing to Thee, and do Thou enkindle within my cold heart the fire of that burning love which Jesus, My Savior, came to cast upon the earth. Amen.

Our Father. Hail Mary. Glory be.

VIII. LITANY OF THE HOLY GHOST

Lord, have mercy on us.
 Christ, have mercy on us.
Lord, have mercy on us.
 Christ, have mercy on us.
Holy Ghost, hear us.
 Holy Ghost, graciously hear us.

God the Father of heaven,
God the Son, Redeemer of the world,
God the Holy Ghost,
Holy Trinity, one God,
Holy Ghost, Who proceedest from the
 Father and the Son,
Holy Ghost, co-equal with the Father and
 the Son,
Promise of the Father, most loving and
 most bounteous,

Have mercy on us.

Gift of the most high God,
Ray of heavenly light,
Author of all good,
Source of living water,
Consuming fire,
Burning love,
Spiritual unction,
Spirit of truth and of power,
Spirit of wisdom and of understanding,
Spirit of counsel and of fortitude,
Spirit of knowledge and of piety,
Spirit of the fear of the Lord,
Spirit of compunction and of penance,
Spirit of grace and of prayer,
Spirit of charity, peace and joy,
Spirit of patience, longanimity and
    goodness,
Spirit of benignity, mildness and fidelity,
Spirit of modesty, continence and
    chastity,
Spirit of adoption of the sons of God,
Holy Ghost, the Comforter,
Holy Ghost, the Sanctifier,
Who in the beginning didst move over
    the waters,
By whose inspirations spake the holy man
    of God,
Who didst overshadow Mary,
Who didst cooperate in the miraculous
    conception of the Son of God,

Have
mercy
on us.

Who didst descend upon Him at His
    baptism,
Who on the Day of Pentecost didst
      appear in fiery tongues upon the
      disciples of the Lord,
By Whom we also are born,
Who dwellest in us,
Who governest the Church,
Who fillest the whole world,

} Have mercy on us.

Holy Ghost,
That Thou renew the face of the earth,
That Thou shed abroad Thy light in our
    hearts,
That Thou write Thy law in our hearts,
That Thou inflame us with the fire of Thy
    love,
That Thou open to us the treasures of Thy
    grace,
That Thou teach us to ask for them
    according to Thy will,
That Thou enlighten us with Thy heav-
    enly inspirations,
That Thou keep us to Thyself by Thy
    powerful attractions,
That Thou grant to us the knowledge
    alone necessary,
That Thou help us to love and bear with
    one another,
That Thou lead us in the way of Thy
    commandments,

} We beseech Thee to hear us.

That Thou make us obedient to Thy
      inspirations,
That Thou teach us to pray, and Thyself
      pray with us,
That Thou clothe us with love towards
      our brethren,
That Thou inspire us with a horror of
      evil,
That Thou direct us in the practice of
      good,
That Thou give us the grace of all virtues,
That Thou cause us to persevere in justice,
That Thou be Thyself our everlasting
      reward,

We beseech Thee to hear us.

Lamb of God, Who takest away the sins of the world,
      Spare us, O Lord.
Lamb of God, Who takest away the sins of the world,
      Graciously hear us, O Lord.
Lamb of God, Who takest away the sins of the world,
      Have mercy on us, O Lord.
Holy Ghost, hear us,
Holy Ghost, graciously hear us.
Lord, have mercy on us,
Christ, have mercy on us,
Lord, have mercy on us.
V. Create in us a clean heart, O God.
R. And renew a right spirit within us.

Let us pray.

Grant, O Merciful Father, that Thy Divine Spirit may enlighten, inflame, and cleanse our hearts; that He may penetrate us with His heavenly dew, and make us fruitful in good works. Through Jesus Christ Our Lord. Amen.

IX. LITTLE OFFICE OF THE HOLY GHOST

At Matins

May the grace of the Holy Ghost enlighten our minds and our hearts. Amen.

V. O Lord, open Thou my lips,

R. And my mouth shall declare Thy praise.

V. Incline unto mine aid, O God.

R. O Lord make haste to help me.

Glory be to the Father, and to the Son, and to the Holy Ghost.

As it was in the beginning, is now, and ever shall be, world without end. Amen.

Alleluia, *or* Praise be to Thee, O Lord, King of Eternal glory. (*From Septuagesima to Holy Thursday.*)

The Hymn

From the rippling of the river,
From the waving Tree of Life,
Gabriel came, a fiery splendor,
Came from God to Joseph's wife.

When with spirit, strong and tender,
Low he knelt in Mary's cell,
In the wondrous work of ages,
Jesus came with us to dwell.

Antiphon. Come, O Holy Ghost, fill the hearts of Thy faithful, and kindle in them the fire of Thy love.

V. Send forth Thy Spirit, and they shall be created.

R. And Thou shall renew the face of the earth.

Let us pray:

May the power of the Holy Ghost be ever with us, we beseech Thee, O God, and may He, in His mercy, cleanse our hearts, and save us from all dangers. Through our Lord Jesus Christ, Who liveth and reigneth with Thee, in the unity of the same Holy Ghost, one God, world without end. Amen.

At Lauds

May the grace of the Holy Ghost enlighten our minds and our hearts. Amen.

V. Incline unto mine aid, O God.
R. O Lord, make haste to help me.
Glory, etc.

The Hymn

Angels, kneeling by the Manger,
　　Gazed upon the kingly Child;
Jesus, born of Virgin-Mother,
　　Looked up in her face and smiled.

Through long years He dwelt with Mary
　　In the Holy Home unseen;
Waiting for the time appointed
　　Lived the lowly Nazarene.

Ant. Come, Holy Ghost, etc., with the prayer as before.

At Prime

May the grace of the Holy Ghost enlighten our minds and our hearts. Amen.

V. Incline unto mine aid, O God,
R. O Lord, make haste to help me.
Glory, etc.

The Hymn

On He went with blessings laden
　　In His sweetness and His might;

And the souls that lay in darkness
　　Saw the shining of His light.

Crucified and dead, He slumbered
　　Sweetly in His Garden Grave:
In His risen light ascending
　　Blessings to His own He gave.

Ant. Come, Holy Ghost, etc., with the prayer as before.

At Terce

May the grace of the Holy Ghost enlighten our minds and our hearts. Amen.

V. Incline unto mine aid, O God.

R. O Lord, make haste to help me.

Glory, etc.

The Hymn

After ten long days of waiting
　　Came the Spirit from above;
For He would not leave them orphans,
　　And He brought them gifts of love.

Fount of Truth and light and healing,
　　With His gifts that Spirit came;
Then the tongues of cloven brightness
　　Swiftly set their hearts on flame.

Ant. Come, Holy Ghost, etc., with the prayer as before.

At Sext

May the grace of the Holy Ghost enlighten our minds and our hearts. Amen.

V. Incline unto mine aid, O God.

R. O Lord, make haste to help me.

Glory, etc.

The Hymn

Then the sevenfold grace descended;
    With it all their souls were filled;
And they gave their Master's message,
    Speaking as the Spirit willed.

Forth they went, in light and gladness,
    Never ceasing, never dim;
Leaving every love for Jesus,
    Giving every love to Him.

Ant. Come, Holy Ghost, etc., with prayer as before.

At None

May the grace of the Holy Ghost enlighten our minds and our hearts. Amen.

V. Incline unto mine aid, O God.

R. O Lord, make haste to help me. Glory, etc.

The Hymn

Reigneth over all the Spirit
>Of the Father and the Son;
Yet in lowly hearts He dwelleth
>'Till the work of God is done.

Balsam of the true Physician,
>Always, Holy Ghost, Thou art;
Healing every pain and sorrow,
>Giving joy to every heart.

Ant. Come, Holy Ghost, etc., with prayer as before.

At Vespers

May the grace of the Holy Ghost enlighten our minds and our hearts. Amen.

V. Incline unto mine aid, O God.

R. O Lord, make haste to help me. Glory, etc.

The Hymn

Now the shades of evening deepen,
>Now the night comes on apace;
Holy Spirit, give Thy servants
>Thoughts of fire and gifts of grace.

Thou dost shine on those who love Thee
>Through the darkness of the light
Holy Spirit, be our Helper,
>Be our Everlasting Light.

Ant. Come, Holy Ghost, etc., with prayer as before.

At Compline

May the grace of the Holy Ghost enlighten our minds and our hearts. Amen.

V. Convert us, O God, our Savior.
R. And turn away Thine anger from us.
V. Incline unto mine aid, O God.
R. O Lord, make haste to help me.
Glory, etc.

The Hymn

May the Spirit, dwelling in us,
    As the noonday, bright and clear,
Fill the souls of all His servants
    Full of love and holy fear,

So when Jesus comes to judgment,
    And before His throne we stand,
Words of gracious love will bring us
    Safely to the Promised Land.

Ant. Come, Holy Ghost, etc., with prayer as before.

The Commendation

These prayers, Eternal Spirit, I have offered to Thee, loving Thee and praising Thee, and adoring Thee, in Thy beauty and majesty, in Thy light and in Thy strength, I pray, Divine Spirit, that Thou wilt always visit us with Thy inspirations and guide us by Thy counsel, that one day we may dwell with Thee forever in the Heavenly Kingdom. Amen.

X. CHAPLET OF THE HOLY GHOST

1. Notice on the Chaplet of the Holy Ghost

The devout exercise in honor of the Divine Spirit, known as the "Chaplet of the Holy Ghost" is proposed to the faithful with a view to its becoming in regard to the Holy Ghost, the third Person of the Most Blessed Trinity, what the Rosary is in regard to Mary, His Immaculate Spouse. It is intended to familiarize men's minds with the mysterious workings of the Divine Spirit, not only in the Church at large, but especially in the individual soul of each of its members, and thus make them more conscious of His patient and loving indwelling, and more ready to follow His Divine Inspirations.

The Chaplet is composed of five mysteries, embodying the chief operations of the Holy Ghost. The number five has been chosen for a particular reason. The principal work of the Holy Ghost on earth is to glorify Jesus by applying to the souls of men the infinite merits of the Divine Redeemer purchased for us by his bitter Passion and Death. The number five reminds you, therefore, of the five wounds of Jesus Christ which are as five fountains out of which the Holy Ghost draws the grace and blessings He imparts to your soul. Hence in meditating upon the operations of the Holy Ghost, your thoughts should be turned to your Crucified Redeemer Who merited for you the graces given you by the Holy Ghost. Hence it is written in Isaias "I will pour out upon the house of David and the inhabitants of Jerusalem the Spirit of grace and of prayers; and they shall look upon Him Whom they have pierced."

By the sevenfold repetition of the "Glory" you are directed to return praise, honor and thanks to the Three Divine Persons for the seven special gifts of the Holy Ghost.

Make it a point to recite this Chaplet frequently. Seriously ponder over the solemn truths it contains and endeavor to put into practice the lessons it conveys. Thus will your devotion to the Holy Ghost assume a particular shape and purpose. You need not recite the whole Chaplet at once. One or other of its mysteries will suffice at a time.

2. Method of reciting the Chaplet

✠ In the name of the Father, and of the Son, and of the Holy Ghost. Amen.

Act of Contrition

O my God, I am very sorry I have sinned against Thee, because Thou art so good, and, by the help of Thy grace, I will not sin again.

Invocation

Come, Holy Ghost, Creator, come
From Thy bright heav'nly throne;
Come, take possession of our souls,
And make them all Thine own.

Thou Who art call'd the Paraclete,
Best gift of God above,
The living spring, the living fire.
Sweet unction and true love.

Thou Who art sevenfold in Thy grace,
Finger of God's right hand;
His promise teaching little ones
To speak and understand.

O, guide our minds with Thy bless'd light,
With love our hearts inflame,
And with Thy strength which ne'er decays,
Confirm our mortal frame.

Far from us drive our deadly foe;
True peace unto us bring,
And through all perils lead us safe
Beneath Thy sacred wing.

Through Thee may we the Father know,
Through Thee th' Eternal Son,
And Thee the Spirit of them both,
Thrice-blessed Three in one.

All glory to the Father be,
With His co-equal Son;
The like to Thee, great Paraclete,
While endless ages run. Amen.

V. Send forth Thy Spirit, and they shall be created.

R. And Thou shalt renew the face of the earth.

Let us pray.

O God, Who didst teach the hearts of Thy faithful by the light of Thy Holy Spirit, grant us, by the same Spirit, to have a right judgment in all things, and evermore to rejoice in His Holy Comfort. Through Jesus Christ, our Lord. Amen.

THE FIRST MYSTERY

By the Holy Ghost is Jesus Conceived of the Virgin Mary

The Meditation: "The Holy Ghost shall come upon thee, and the power of the Most High shall overshadow thee; and therefore also the Holy which shall be born of thee shall be called the Son of God."—*Luke* 1:55.

The Practice: Diligently implore the aid of the Divine Spirit and Mary's intercession to enable you to imitate the virtues of Jesus Christ, the Model of the Elect, so that you may be "made conformable to the image of the Son of God."

Our Father (*once*). Hail Mary (*once*). Glory be (*seven times*).

The Second Mystery

The Spirit of the Lord Rested Upon Jesus

The Meditation: And Jesus being baptized forthwith came out of the water; and lo! the heavens were opened to Him, and He saw the Spirit of God descending as a dove and coming upon Him." —*Matt.* 3:16.

The Practice: Hold in the highest esteem the priceless gift of sanctifying grace infused into your soul by the Holy Ghost in Baptism. Remember to keep the promises to which you then pledged yourself. Preserve and increase, by constant practice, the virtues of Faith, Hope and Charity. Ever live as becometh a child of God and a member of God's true Church, so as to obtain, hereafter, your heavenly inheritance.

Our Father (*once*). Hail Mary (*once*). Glory be (*seven times*).

The Third Mystery

By the Spirit is Jesus Led into the Desert to be Tempted

The Meditation: "And Jesus being full of the Holy Ghost returned from the Jordan, and was led by the Spirit into the desert, for the space of forty days, and was tempted by the devil."—*Luke* 4:1–2.

The Practice: Be ever grateful for the sevenfold gift of the Holy Ghost bestowed upon you in Confirmation—wisdom, understanding, counsel, fortitude, knowledge, piety, and fear of the Lord. Faithfully yield yourself to His Divine guidance so that, in all the trials and temptations to which you are exposed in passing through the desert of this world, you may act manfully, as becometh a perfect Christian and a true soldier of Jesus Christ.

Our Father (*once*). Hail Mary (*once*). Glory be (*seven times*).

THE FOURTH MYSTERY

The Abiding Presence of the Holy Ghost in the Church

The Meditation: "And suddenly there came a sound from heaven as of a mighty wind coming, and it filled the whole house where they were sitting and they were all filled with the Holy Ghost, and began to speak the wonderful works of God."—*Acts* 2:1, 4, 11.

The Practice: Thank God for belonging to His true Church which is ever animated and directed by His Divine Spirit, sent into the world for that purpose on the Day of Pentecost. Be devoted to the Holy See, the infallible mouthpiece of the Holy Ghost. Hear and obey the Church, the pillar and ground of Truth. Uphold her doctrines, seek her interests, defend her rights.

Our Father (*once*). Hail Mary (*once*). Glory be (*seven times*).

THE FIFTH MYSTERY

The Abiding Presence of the Holy Ghost Within the Soul of the Just Man

The Meditation: "Know ye not that your members are the temple of the Holy Ghost, Who is in you?" —*1 Cor.* 6:19. "Extinguish not the Spirit."—*1 Thess.* 5:19. "And grieve not the Spirit of God whereby you are sealed unto the day of redemption."—*Eph.* 4:30.

The Practice: Be ever mindful of the personal presence of the Holy Ghost within you, and carefully cultivate purity of soul and body. Strive also to faithfully correspond with His Divine Inspirations, that, by so doing, you may bring forth, in your soul, the most holy Fruit of the Spirit, which is "Charity, joy, peace, patience, benignity, goodness, longanimity, mildness, faith, modesty, continency, chastity."—*Galat.* 5:22.

Our Father (*once*). Hail Mary (*once*). Glory be (*seven times*).

Conclude with the I believe, as a profession of Faith.

Say finally Our Father (*once*) and Hail Mary (*once*), for the intentions of the Sovereign Pontiff.

3. Method of public recital of the Chaplet

✠ In the name of the Father, and of the Son, and of the Holy Ghost. Amen.

An Act of Contrition

O my God, I am very sorry I have sinned against Thee because Thou art so good, and, by the help of Thy grace, I will not sin again.

Invocation

Come, O Holy Ghost, fill the hearts of Thy faithful, and kindle in them the fire of Thy love.

V. Send forth Thy Spirit, and they shall be created.

R. And Thou shall renew the face of the earth.

Let us pray:

O God, Who didst teach the hearts of Thy faithful by the light of Thy Holy Spirit, grant us, by the same Spirit, to have a right judgment in all things, and evermore to rejoice in His Holy Comfort, through Jesus Christ, our Lord, Amen.

I.

Hymn

(Said or Sung.)
Come, Holy Ghost, Creator, come
From Thy bright heav'nly throne:
Come, take possession of our souls,
And make them all Thine own.

THE FIRST MYSTERY

By the Holy Ghost is Jesus Conceived of the Virgin Mary

Let us contemplate in this mystery the wondrous work of the Holy Ghost in Mary, amending as it is written: "The Holy Ghost shall come upon thee, and the power of the Most High shall overshadow thee; and therefore also the Holy which shall be born of thee shall be called the Son of God."—*Luke* 1:35.

Let us diligently implore the aid of the Divine Spirit, and Mary's intercession, that we may be enabled to imitate Jesus Christ, the Model of the Elect, so that we may "be made conformable to the image of the Son of God."

Our Father (*once*). Hail Mary (*once*). Glory be (*seven times*).

Let us pray:

O God, whose only Begotten Son was made manifest in the substance of our flesh, mercifully grant that our inward man may be changed into the likeness of Him Whose outward Man is made like unto us; even the same our Lord Jesus Christ Thy Son, Who liveth and reigneth with Thee, in the unity of the Holy Ghost, one God, world without end. Amen.

(Prayer for Sunday within the octave of Epiphany.)

II.

Hymn

(Said or Sung.)
Thou Who art called the Paraclete,
Best Gift of God above,
The living spring, the living fire,
Sweet unction, and true love.

The Second Mystery

The Spirit of the Lord Rested Upon Jesus

Let us contemplate in this mystery how: "Jesus, being baptized, came out of the water, and lo! the heavens were opened to Him, and He saw the Spirit of God descending as a dove, and coming upon Him." —*Matt.* 3:11.

Let us hold in the highest esteem the priceless gift of sanctifying grace infused into our soul by the Holy Ghost in Baptism. Let us remember to keep the promises to which we then pledged ourselves. Let us preserve and increase, by constant practice, the virtues of Faith, Hope, and Charity. Let us ever live as becometh children of God, and members of God's true Church, so as to obtain, hereafter, our heavenly inheritance.

Our Father (*once*). Hail Mary (*once*). Glory be (*seven times*).

Let us pray:

Grant, we beseech Thee, O Almighty God, that the splendor of Thy brightness may shine forth upon us, and that the light of Thy Light may, by the illumination of the Holy Spirit, confirm the hearts of them that have, by Thy grace, been regenerated; through our Lord Jesus Christ Thy Son, Who liveth and reigneth with Thee, in the unity of the same Holy Ghost, one God, world without end. Amen.

(Prayer for Whit Sunday evening.)

III.

Hymn

(Said or Sung.)
Thou Who art sevenfold in Thy grace,
Finger of God's right hand;
His Promise, teaching little ones
To speak and understand.

THE THIRD MYSTERY

By the Spirit is Jesus Led into the Desert to be Tempted

Let us contemplate, how "Jesus being full of the Holy Ghost returned from the Jordan, and was led by the Spirit into the desert, for the space of forty days, and was tempted by the devil."—*Luke* 4:1–2.

Let us be ever grateful for the sevenfold gift of the Holy Ghost bestowed upon us in confirmation, wisdom, understanding, counsel, fortitude, knowledge, piety, and fear of the Lord. Let us faithfully yield ourselves to His Divine guidance, so that, in all the trials and temptations to which we are exposed in passing through the desert of this world, we may act manfully as becometh perfect Christians and true soldiers of Jesus Christ.

Our Father (*once*). Hail Mary (*once*). Glory be (*seven times*).

Let us pray:

Grant, we beseech Thee, O Almighty God, that we may deserve the Holy Spirit by assiduous prayers, so that, by His grace, we may both be delivered from all temptations and merit to obtain the pardon of our sins; through our Lord Jesus Christ Thy Son, Who liveth and reigneth with Thee, in the unity of the same Holy Ghost, one God, world without end. Amen.

(Second Post Communion of the Votive Mass of the Holy Ghost.)

IV.

Hymn

(*Said or Sung.*)
O, guide our minds with Thy Bless'd light,
With love our hearts inflame,
And with Thy strength which ne'er decays,
Confirm our mortal frame.

The Fourth Mystery

The Abiding Presence of the Holy Ghost in the Church

Let us contemplate how, on the day of Pentecost, "there suddenly came a sound from heaven as of a mighty wind coming, and it filled the whole house where they were sitting and they were filled with the Holy Ghost and began to speak the wonderful works of God."—*Acts* 2:1, 4, 11.

Let us thank God for belonging to His true Church which is ever animated and directed by his Divine Spirit, sent into the world for that purpose on the day of Pentecost. Let us be devoted to the Holy See, the infallible mouthpiece of the Holy Ghost. Let us hear and obey the Church, the pillar and ground of Truth. Let us uphold her doctrines, seek her interests, defend her rights.

Our Father (*once*). Hail Mary (*once*). Glory be (*seven times*).

Let us pray:

O Almighty and everlasting God, by Whose Spirit the whole body of the Church is sanctified and governed: receive our humble supplications which we offer before Thee for all degrees and orders of men in Thy

Holy Church, that, by the inheritance of Thy grace, they may serve Thee faithfully; through our Lord Jesus Christ Thy Son, Who liveth and reigneth with Thee, in the unity of the same Holy Ghost one God, world without end. Amen.

V.

Hymn

(Said or Sung.)
Far from us drive our deadly foe;
True peace unto us bring;
And through all perils lead us safe
Beneath thy sacred wing.

THE FIFTH MYSTERY

The Abiding Presence of the Holy Ghost in the Soul of the Just Man

Let us contemplate in this mystery the Divine Presence of the Divine Spirit within our souls and bodies, according as it is written: "Know ye not that your members are the temple of the Holy Ghost Who is in you?"—*1 Cor.* 6:19. "Extinguish not the Spirit" —*1 Thess.* 5:19. "And grieve not the Holy Spirit of God

whereby you are sealed unto the day of redemption."
—*Eph.* 4:30.

"Let us be ever mindful of the personal presence of the Holy Ghost within us and carefully cultivate purity of soul and body. Let us strive also to faithfully correspond with His Divine Inspirations, that, by so doing, we may bring forth, in our soul, the most holy Fruit of the Spirit which is charity, joy, peace, patience, benignity, goodness, longanimity, mildness, faith, modesty, continency, chastity."—*Galat.* 5:22.

Our Father (*once*). Hail Mary (*once*). Glory be (*seven times*).

Let us pray:

May the infusion of the Holy Spirit cleanse our hearts, O Lord, and render them fruitful by the inward watering of His heavenly dew; through our Lord Jesus Christ Thy Son, Who liveth and reigneth with Thee, in the unity of the same Holy Ghost, one God, world without end. Amen.

(Post Communion of the Mass on Whit Sunday.)

Hymn

(Said or Sung.)
Through Thee may we the Father know,
Through Thee th' Eternal Son,

And Thee the Spirit of them both,
Thrice-blessed Three in one.

Our Father (*once*). Hail Mary (*once*). Glory be (*seven times*).

Conclude with the I believe as a profession of Faith. Say finally one Our Father for the intention of the Sovereign Pontiff.

Let us pray:

O God, the Pastor and Ruler of all the faithful, look down, in Thy mercy, upon Thy servant—(here mention the Pope's name) whom Thou hast appointed to preside over Thy Church; and grant, we beseech Thee, that both by word and example he may edify all those who are under his charge; so that, with the flock entrusted to him, he may arrive at length unto life everlasting; through our Lord Jesus Christ Thy Son, who liveth and reigneth with Thee, in the unity of the Holy Ghost, one God, world without end. Amen.

Hymn

(Said or Sung.)
All glory to the Father be,
With His co-equal Son;
The like to Thee, great Paraclete,
While endless ages run.
                              Amen.

4. Brief Reflections on the five Mysteries of the Chaplet

The First Mystery reminds you of the fact that it was through the Power of the Holy Ghost that the Incarnation of the Son of God was effected in Mary. And since none can be saved unless he "be made conformable to the image of the Son of God," implore the Divine Spirit, that through the intercession of Mary, His Immaculate Spouse, He may, by His grace, produce within you this Divine likeness.

The Second Mystery brings before your mind the Baptism of Jesus as an emblem of your own. For at your baptism, God the Father accepted you as His child, and God the Holy Ghost descended upon you to enrich your soul with His Divine gifts. Be mindful, therefore, to value and esteem the favors conferred on you in Baptism, so as to keep the promises to which you then pledged yourself.

The Third Mystery shows you the special influence of the Holy Ghost upon the Sacred Manhood of Jesus Christ, and thus reminds you how you, likewise, must allow yourself to be guided in all things by the same Divine Spirit, who came to you again in Confirmation with the plentitude of His gifts, to make you a strong and perfect Christian and soldier of Jesus Christ. Hence, be ever mindful of the graces received in Confirmation and faithfully correspond with them, so as to overcome all temptations and successfully carry out the particular work for which God has placed you on this earth.

The Fourth Mystery brings before your mind the special office of the Holy Ghost in the Body of the Church, whose life-giving principle He became on the Day of Pentecost, and in which He will abide as such to the end of time. Resolve, therefore, to be always and everywhere a humble, docile, and zealous member of the Church; for by her infallible teachings are you enabled to live in the true Faith, by her Divine ministry are you strengthened with every grace, and by her sacred government are you placed on the right road to heaven.

The Fifth and Last Mystery brings before your mind the office of the Holy Ghost in your own individual soul. By His mysterious indwelling, your body has become His living Temple and your soul His living Sanctuary. Strive, therefore, after purity of body and soul. Beware, lest by grievous sin, you should ever drive this Divine Guest from your soul. Take care, also, never to grieve Him, by wilfully falling into deliberate venial sins. In all your thoughts, words and actions keep His Divine Presence before your eyes, so that the fruit of His patient indwelling may show themselves in the garden of your soul.

5. Acts of Praise and Thanksgiving

✠ In the name of the Father, and of the Son, and of the Holy Ghost. Amen.

O Divine Spirit, Substantial Love of the Father, and of the Son, deign to make me worthy to sing Thy praises for ever more!

I.

All praise, thanksgiving and glory be given to God the Holy Ghost Who overshadowed Mary, His Immaculate Spouse, Mother of God, and by Whom "The Word was made Flesh," and a Savior given unto us. Amen.

Glory be to the Father, and to the Son, and to the Holy Ghost.

As it was in the beginning, is now, and ever shall be, world without end. Amen.

II.

All praise, thanksgiving and glory be given to God the Holy Ghost Who, at Baptism made us the adopted Sons of God, filled our hearts with His sanctifying grace and imparted to us the supernatural gifts of Faith, Hope and Charity and the seed of every virtue. Amen.

Glory.

III.

All praise, thanksgiving and glory be given to God the Holy Ghost Who, at Confirmation, sealed our souls unto God and made us strong and perfect Christians and soldiers of Jesus Christ, fortifying us with His seven fold gift of wisdom and of understanding, of counsel and of knowledge, of fortitude and of piety, and of the fear of the Lord. Amen.

Glory.

IV.

All praise, thanksgiving and glory be given to God the Holy Ghost, Who descending upon the Apostles and Disciples on the Day of Pentecost, became the Life and Life-giver of the Church, by whose teaching He makes known to us all truth, by whose Sacraments He gives us grace, and by whose guidance He directs us on the way to heaven. Amen.

Glory.

V.

All praise, thanksgiving and glory be given to God the Holy Ghost Who, by His personal indwelling in our souls and bodies, sanctifies and consecrates unto God our entire being, enabling us to think holily, speak holily and act holily, and to produce His Divine fruit:

charity, joy, peace, patience, benignity, goodness, longanimity, mildness, faith, modesty, continency, chastity. Amen.

Glory.

XI. Devout Exercises in honor of God the Holy Ghost for each day in the week

If possible, devote a few spare moments each day of the week to honor the Holy Ghost. For this purpose, the following exercises are proposed to you. The words are chosen from Sacred Scripture, and are therefore the inspired words of God the Holy Ghost Himself. Read them slowly, attentively and devoutly, and make such aspirations as will suggest themselves to you. Before each exercise, make the sign of the Cross, place yourself in the presence of God, and make an act of contrition.

1. Sunday—Adoration

The Spirit of the Lord hath filled the whole world: Come, let us adore Him!

The Holy Ghost:—I am Alpha and Omega: the beginning and the end. I am the Lord; that make all things, that stretch out I the heavens and establish the earth, and there is none but Me.

I am the Lord, thy God. Thou shalt not have strange gods before Me. Thou shalt not take the name of the Lord, thy God, in vain. Remember, thou keep holy the Sabbath-day.

I am the Almighty God: walk before Me, and be perfect.

The Soul:—Great and wonderful are Thy works, O Lord, God Almighty; just and true are Thy ways, O King of Ages.

Whither shall I go from Thy Spirit? or whither shall I flee from Thy face? If I ascend into heaven, Thou art there. If I descend into hell, Thou art present. If I take my wings early in the morning, and dwell in the uttermost parts of the sea: even there also shall Thy hand lead me, and Thy right hand hold me. And I said: Perhaps darkness shall cover me: and night shall be my light in my pleasures. But darkness shall not be darkness to Thee, and night shall be light as the day.

Of Him, and by Him, and in Him are all things.

Holy! Holy! Holy! Lord God of Hosts. The whole earth is full of Thy glory.

Glory be to the Father! Glory be to the Son! Glory be to the Holy Ghost! Amen.

Aspiration:—May the grace of the Holy Ghost enlighten our minds and hearts. Amen.

Invocation:—Come, O Holy Spirit! fill the hearts of Thy faithful; and kindle in them the fire of Thy love.

Practice:—Make it a rule to invoke the aid of the Holy Ghost before each of your undertakings, spiritual or temporal.

2. Monday—Esteem

The Spirit of the Lord hath filled the whole world: Come, let us adore Him.

The Holy Ghost:—I will give them one heart, and will put a new spirit in their bowels. I will take away the stony heart out of their flesh, and will give them a heart of flesh: that they may walk in My commandments, and keep My judgments and do them; and that they may be My people, and I may be their God.

It shall come to pass that I will pour out My Spirit upon all flesh; and your sons and daughters shall prophecy, your old men shall dream dreams, and your young men shall see visions. Moreover, upon My servants and handmaids in those days I will pour forth My Spirit.

There are diversities of graces, but the same Spirit.

The fruit of the Spirit is charity, joy, peace, patience, benignity, goodness, longanimity, mildness, faith, modesty, continency, chastity.

The Soul:—O the depth of the riches, of the power, of the wisdom, and of the knowledge of God! How incomprehensible are His judgments, and how unsearchable His ways!

Who hath known the mind of the Lord? or who hath been His counsellor? Who hath first given Him, and recompense shall be made him?

Of Him, and by Him, and in Him are all things. To Him be glory, now and for evermore. Amen.

Aspiration:—Create in me a clean heart, O God; and renew a right spirit within me.

Invocation:—Come, O Holy Spirit, and so take possession of my whole being as to direct all my thoughts, words, and actions.

Practice:—Be grateful to the Holy Ghost for the many graces He daily bestows upon you. Faithfully correspond with them, and serve Him with a clean mind and a pure heart.

3. Tuesday—Joy

The Spirit of the Lord hath filled the whole world: Come, let us adore Him!

The Holy Ghost:—I have loved thee with an everlasting love; wherefore have I drawn thee, taking pity on thee.

I am He that blot out thy iniquities, and I will not remember thy sins.

Thou shalt know that the Lord, thy God, is a strong and faithful Cod, keeping His covenant and mercy to them that love Him, and to them that keep His commandments unto a thousand generations.

The Lord is sweet to all, and His tender mercies are over all His works.

Many are the scourges of the sinner; but mercy shall encompass him that hopeth in the Lord.

In a moment of indignation have I hidden My face a little while from thee; but with everlasting kindness have I had mercy on thee.

The Soul:—Thou sparest all, because they are Thine, O Lord, Who lovest souls!

O how good and sweet is Thy Spirit, O Lord, in all things!

Thou chastisest them that err, little by little, and admonishest them, and speakest to them concerning the things, wherein they offend, that leaving their wickedness, they may believe in Thee, O Lord.

Aspiration:—Thou hast given gladness to my heart, O God. Let all them be glad, that hope in Thee.

Invocation:—Restore unto me the joy of Thy salvation, and strengthen me with a perfect spirit.

Practice:—Hate and detest sin as the greatest evil. Carefully shun all dangerous occasions of sin. Be constant in the regular practice of Confession. Then shall you keep your mind and heart at peace in the joy of the Holy Ghost.

4. Wednesday—Grief

The Spirit of the Lord hath filled the whole world: Come, let us adore Him!

The Holy Ghost:—Behold My delights are to be with the children of men. And My people have forsaken Me. My foolish people have not known Me. Why have you forsaken the Lord! With desolation is all the land made desolate, because there is none that considereth in the heart.

Behold, My delights are to be with the children of men. And He (Jesus) came unto His own, and His own received Him not. O ye sons of men, how long will ye be dull of heart? Why do ye love vanity and seek after lying? In that day ye shall be desolate, because ye have forgotten God, your Savior.

Behold, My delights are to be with the children of men. I have spread forth My hands all the day to an unbelieving people, who walk in a way that is not good after their own thoughts. I looked for one that would grieve together with Me, and I found none.

I came to cast fire on the earth, and what would I, but that it be enkindled? Will you also go away?

The Soul:—Lord, Thou knowest all things. Thou knowest that I love Thee. What have I in heaven? and besides Thee, what do I desire upon earth? For Thee, my heart and my flesh hath fainted away. Thou art the God of my heart, and the God that is my portion forever.

Thou art worthy, O Lord our God, to receive honor, and glory, and power. O God, my God, for Thee do I watch at break of day. For Thee my soul hath thirsted; for Thee my flesh how many ways!

My Lord and my God! Impute not to me my iniquity, nor remember the injuries of Thy servant. For I, Thy servant, acknowledge my sin. If I would justify myself, my own mouth shall condemn me. Hear the prayer of Thy servant while I pray before Thee now, night and day, for the children of Israel, Thy servants.

Aspiration:—Cast me not away from Thy face; and take not Thy Holy Spirit from me!

Invocation:—Blessed be God, Who hath not turned away my prayer, nor His mercy from me.

Practice:—So grieve over your sins and failings as to mend your ways and root out all evil habits.

5. Thursday—Thanksgiving

The Spirit of the Lord hath filled the whole world: Come, let us adore Him!

The Holy Ghost:—In everything, by prayer and supplication, with Thanksgiving, let your petitions be made known to God.

Be filled with the Holy Ghost, giving thanks always.

Were not ten made clean? And where are the nine?

The Son honoreth the Father, and the servant his Master. If then, I be a Father, where is My honor? And if I be a Master, where is my fear? saith the Lord of Hosts. Is this the return thou makest to the Lord, O foolish and senseless people?

The hope of the ungrateful shall melt away, as the winter's ice.

Know this, that, in the last days, shall come danger-ous times. Men shall be lovers of themselves, covetous, haughty, proud, blasphemous, disobedient, wicked, ungrateful.

The Soul:—Bless the Lord, O my soul, and forget not all He hath done for thee; Who forgiveth all thy iniqui-ties; Who healeth all thy diseases; Who redeemeth thy life from destruction; Who covereth thee with mercy and compassion.

I will praise Thee, O Lord, with my whole heart: I will narrate all Thy wonders. I will be glad and rejoice in Thee: I will sing to Thy name. I will give thanks to Thee, O Lord, for Thou wast angry with me: Thy wrath is turned away, and Thou hast comforted me.

We give thanks to Thee our God, and we praise Thy glorious Name.

Aspiration:—Thanks be to God for His unspeakable Gift.

Invocation:—O my God, grant me to understand and value more and more that gift above all the other gifts, Thy Divine Spirit Who has been poured abroad in our hearts.

Practice:—As far as you can, spread among others devotion to the Holy Ghost so that He may be known and loved by men more and more.

6. Friday—Condolence

The Spirit of the Lord hath filled the whole world: Come, let us adore Him!

The Holy Ghost:—I will pour out upon the house of David, and upon the inhabitants of Jerusalem, the Spirit of grace, and of prayer. And they shall look upon Me whom they have pierced.

They shall mourn for Him as one mourneth for an only Son; and they shall grieve over Him, as the manner is to grieve for the death of the first-born.

I have opened forth My hands all the day to an unbelieving people.

O my people, what have I done to thee, or in what have I molested thee? Answer thou me.

Father, forgive them; for they know not what they do.—Amen I say to thee, this day, thou shalt be with me in paradise.—Woman, behold thy Son . . . Son, behold thy mother!—My God, My God! Why hast Thou forsaken Me?—I thirst.—It is consummated.—Father, into Thy hand I commend My Spirit.

O, all ye that pass by the way, attend and see if there be any sorrow like unto My sorrow.

The Soul:—Who will give water to my head, and a fountain of tears to my eyes? My eye hath run down with streams of water.

God forbid that I should glory, save in the Cross of the Lord Jesus Christ, by whom the world is crucified to me, and I to the world.

With Christ, I am nailed to the Cross.

Lord, remember me, when Thou shalt enter into Thy Kingdom.

Hear me speedily, O Lord. My spirit hath fainted away. My eyes have looked unto Thee before the morning, that I might think upon Thy words.

Father, if Thou wilt, remove this chalice from me, yet not my will, but Thine, he done.

Aspiration:—Gladly will I glory in my infirmities that the power of Christ may dwell in me.

Invocation:—O Divine Spirit, Spirit of grace and of prayer, enable me so to look upon Him Whom I have pierced by my sins that I may detest sin above all things and suffer anything rather than sin again.

Practice:—Out of love for your Crucified Redeemer,

endeavor to bear with patience and courage the crosses and trials of your daily life.

7. Saturday—Petition

The Spirit of the Lord hath filled the whole world: Come, let us adore Him!

The Holy Ghost:—Study wisdom, My son and make My heart joyful.

The work of God on high is the fountain of Wisdom, and her ways are everlasting commandments.

The love of God is honorable Wisdom.

The fear of the Lord is the beginning of Wisdom.

The Wisdom that is from above, first indeed is chaste, then peaceable, modest, easy to be persuaded, consenting to the good, full of mercy and good fruits, without perjury, without dissimulation.

Wisdom will not enter a malicious soul, nor dwell in a body subject to sin. For the Holy Spirit of discipline will flee from the deceitful and will withdraw Himself.

If thou shalt call for Wisdom, she will teach thee temperance and prudence, and justice, and fortitude, which are such things as men can have nothing more profitable on earth.

The Soul:—O Lord, give me Wisdom that sitteth by Thy throne, and cast me not off from among Thy children.

Who shall know Thy thought, O Lord, except Thou give Wisdom, and send Thy Holy Spirit from above.

Send forth Thy Light and Thy Truth. Teach me to do Thy will, for Thou art my God.

Thy good Spirit shall lead me into the right land.

I will meditate on Thee in the morning: and I will rejoice under the covert of Thy Wings.

How sweet are Thy words to my palate: more than honey to my mouth.

Thy word is a lamp to my feet: and a light to my path.

Aspiration:—Blessed is the man whom Thou shalt instruct: and shalt teach him out of Thy law.

Invocation:—O Divine Spirit of Wisdom, teach me to do Thy will; for Thou art my God.

Practice:—From time to time, carefully read, and devoutly meditate upon, Sacred Scripture inspired by the Holy Ghost especially the New Testament. Devote some of your leisure time to useful reading.

XII. THE DIVINE OFFICE FOR PENTECOST SUNDAY

(From the Roman Breviary.)

"Seven times a day I give praise to Thee"

1. Notice

God is to be praised by all men, both privately and publicly. The Church, being the visible body of Christ's redeemed on earth, acknowledges this duty and imposes it upon her priests and the members of her religious orders, so that it becomes their particular office to praise God in the name of all men. It is rightly called the Divine Office. Its object is Divine; for it aims at offering to God here on earth the same homage of praise given Him by His angels and saints in heaven. The very source is Divine: for it consists of portions taken from the sacred Scripture, the inspired word of God; of extracts from the writings of the Holy Fathers, and other parts composed by eminent men at the injunction of the Church. And the whole is so beautifully woven together and harmoniously arranged as to bring vividly before one's eye, throughout the liturgical year, a compendium of all the wonderful works of God, the sorrows and glories of Jesus, our Redeemer, and of His Blessed Mother, the lives and acts of the holy martyrs and saints of God. Nothing can compare with it in sublimity. Nothing can surpass its efficacy. It is the prayer of the entire Church, offered to God in accents inspired directly or indirectly by the Divine Spirit, and offered, moreover, in union with those Divine praises which Jesus, its Divine Head, offered while on earth, and which He still offers in the secrecy of the Tabernacle on the Altar.

The Divine Office is now recited privately by all priests, but is also still publicly chanted in many places, especially in houses of religious orders. In former times the laity would piously assist at all the canonical hours, especially on feast days. Now at most Vespers, and sometimes Compline, are sung publicly on Sundays and holy days to enable the faithful to take part in this public form of prayer.

Yet why not take up the Breviary as a manual of private devotions? No doubt the ordinary occupations of secular life leave little time to say the whole office each day. But a small portion of it could easily be recited occasionally. Where, for instance, will you find a more beautiful form of morning prayer than in the office of Prime, or of night prayer than in the office of Compline?

Here we propose as a special devotion in honor of God the Holy Ghost the Divine Office appointed to be said on Pentecost Sunday. It forms a most suitable exercise of devotion, especially during Whitsun-tide. It need not be said all in one day. As there are seven parts, one could be recited each day of the week. The office for Pentecost is given here just as it stands in the Breviary, and slightly differs from the other offices of the year. All rubrics or particular directions are omitted, as it is meant for private use.

During the recital of the Divine Office you should occupy your mind with some good and profitable thoughts. The very idea of the festival you celebrate and the meaning of the words you utter will of themselves supply you with ample food for reflection. The antiphon said before and after each psalm gives that psalm its special meaning and shows you how to adapt it to the particular occasion.

2. Prayer before Divine Office

Open, O Lord, my mouth, to bless Thy holy name; cleanse also my heart from all vain, perverse, and distracting thoughts; enlighten my understanding, influence my will, that I may worthily, attentively, and devoutly recite this holy office, and deserve to be heard in the presence of Thy Divine Majesty. Through Christ, our Lord. Amen.

O Lord, I offer up to Thee these hours, in unison with that divine intention, with which Thou Thyself, while on earth, didst render to God the homage of praise.

3. Matins and Lauds

OUR FATHER, who art in heaven, hallowed be Thy name: Thy Kingdom come: Thy will be done on earth as it is in heaven. Give us this day our daily bread: and forgive us our trespasses as we forgive them that trespass against us. And lead us not into temptation: but deliver us from evil. Amen.

HAIL, MARY, full of grace: the Lord is with thee: blessed art thou among women, and blessed is the fruit of thy womb, Jesus. Holy Mary, mother of God, pray for us sinners, now and at the hour of our death. Amen.

I BELIEVE in God, the Father Almighty, Creator of heaven and earth; and in Jesus Christ, His only Son, our Lord, Who was conceived by the Holy Ghost, born of the Virgin Mary, suffered under Pontius Pilate, was crucified; died, and was buried. He descended into hell; the third day He arose again from the dead; He ascended into heaven, sitteth at the right hand of God the Father Almighty; from thence He shall come to judge the living and the dead. I believe in the Holy Ghost, the Holy Catholic Church, the communion of Saints, the forgiveness of sins, the resurrection of the body, and life everlasting. Amen.

V. O Lord, open Thou my lips.

R. And my mouth shall declare Thy praise.

V. Incline unto mine aid, O God.

R. O Lord, make haste to help me.

Glory be to the Father, and to the Son, and to the Holy Ghost: As it was in the beginning, is now, and ever shall be, world without end. Amen. Alleluia.

The Invitatory

Alleluia. The Spirit of the Lord hath filled the whole world: Come, let us adore! Alleluia.

Alleluia. The Spirit of the Lord hath filled the whole world: Come, let us adore! Alleluia.

Psalm 94

Come, let us praise the Lord with joy, let us joyfully sing to God our Savior: let us come before His presence with thanksgiving, and make a joyful noise to Him with psalms.

Alleluia. The Spirit of the Lord hath filled the whole world: Come, let us adore! Alleluia.

For the Lord is a great God, and a great King above all gods: The Lord will not cast off His people, for in His hands are all the ends of the earth, and the heights of the mountains He looketh upon.

Come, let us adore! Alleluia.

For the sea is His, and He made it, and His hands formed the dry land: Come, let us adore and fall down before God: let us weep before the Lord, Who made us, for He is the Lord our God; and we are His people and the sheep of His pasture.

Alleluia. The Spirit of the Lord hath filled the whole world: Come, let us adore! Alleluia.

Today, if you shall hear His voice, harden not your hearts, as in the provocation, according to the day of temptation in the wilderness: where your fathers tempted Me, they proved Me and saw My works.

Come, let us adore! Alleluia.

Forty years long was I offended with that generation, and I said: These always err in heart: but these men have not known My ways; so I swore in My wrath that they shall not enter into My rest.

Alleluia. The Spirit of the Lord hath filled the whole world: Come, let us adore! Alleluia.

Glory be to the Father, and to the Son, and to the Holy Ghost: As it was in the beginning, is now, and ever shall be, world without end. Amen.

Come, let us adore! Alleluia.

Alleluia. The Spirit of the Lord hath filled the whole world: Come, let us adore! Alleluia.

The Hymn

Above the starry spheres
    To where He was before
Christ had gone up, soon from on high
    The Father's gift to pour;

And now had fully come,
    On mystic circle borne
Of seven times seven revolving days
    The Pentecostal morn:

When as the Apostles knelt
    At the third hour in prayer,
A sudden rushing sound proclaimed
    The God of glory near.

Forthwith a tongue of fire
    Alights on every brow;
Each breast receives the Father's Light,
    The world's enkindling glow.

The Holy Ghost on all
    Is mightily outpoured;
Who straight in divers tongues declare
    The wonders of the Lord.

While strangers of all climes
    Flock round from far and near.
And with amazement, each at once
    Their native accents hear.

But faithless still, the Jews
    Deny the hand Divine;
And madly jeer the Saints of Christ
    As drunk with new-made wine.

Till Peter in the midst
    Stood up, and spake aloud;
And their perfidious falsity
    By Joel's witness showed.

Praise to the Father be!
    Praise to the Son who rose!
Praise to the Holy Paraclete!
    While age on ages flows.
                Amen.

The Nocturne

Antiphon. Suddenly there came a sound from heaven, as of a mighty wind coming. Alleluia. Alleluia.

Psalm 47

Great is the Lord, and exceedingly to be praised in the city of our God, in His holy mountain.

With the joy of the whole earth is Mount Sion founded, on the sides of the north, the city of the Great King.

In her houses shall God be known, when He shall protect her.

For behold the kings of the earth assembled themselves: they gathered together.

So they saw, and they wondered, they were troubled, they were moved: trembling took hold of them.

There were pains as of a woman in labor. With a vehement wind thou shalt break in pieces the ships of Tharsis.

As we have heard, so have we seen, in the city of the Lord of Hosts, in the city of our God: God hath founded it for ever.

We have received Thy mercy, O God, in the midst of Thy temple.

According to Thy name, O God, so also is Thy praise unto the ends of the earth: Thy right hand is full of justice.

Let Mount Sion rejoice, and the daughters of Juda be glad: because of Thy judgments, O Lord.

Surround Sion, and encompass her: tell ye in her towers.

Set your hearts on her strength; and distribute her houses, that ye may relate it in another generation.

For this is God, our God unto eternity, and for ever and ever: He shall rule us for evermore.

Glory be to the Father, and to the Son, and to the Holy Ghost.

As it was in the beginning, is now, and ever shall be, world without end. Amen.

Antiphon. Suddenly there came a sound from heaven, as of a mighty wind coming. Alleluia. Alleluia.

Antiphon. Confirm, O God, what Thou hast wrought in us: from Thy holy temple which is in Jerusalem. Alleluia. Alleluia.

Psalm 67

Let God arise, and let His enemies be scattered: and let them that hate Him flee from before His face.

As smoke vanisheth, so let them vanish away: as wax melteth before the fire, so let the wicked perish at the presence of God.

And let the just feast, and rejoice before God: and be delighted with gladness.

Sing ye to God, sing a psalm to His name: make a way for Him Who ascendeth upon the west: the Lord is His name.

Rejoice ye before Him: but the wicked shall be troubled at His presence, Who is the father of orphans and the judge of widows.

God in His Holy place: God Who maketh men of one manner to dwell in a house.

Who bringeth out them that were bound in strength: in like manner them that provoke, that dwell in sepulchres.

O God, when Thou didst go forth in the sight of Thy people, when Thou didst pass through the desert:

The earth was moved, and the heavens dropped at the presence of the God of Sinai, at the presence of the God of Israel.

Thou shall set aside for Thy inheritance a free rain, O God: and it was weakened, but Thou hast made it perfect.

In it shall Thy animals dwell; in Thy sweetness, O God, Thou hast provided for the poor.

The Lord shall give the word to them that preach good tidings with great power.

The King of Powers is of the beloved, of the beloved; and the beauty of the house shall divide spoils.

If you sleep among the midst of lots, you shall be as the wings of a dove covered with silver, and the hinder parts of her back with the paleness of gold.

When He that is in heaven appointeth kings over her, they shall be whited with snow in Selmon. The mountain of God is a fat mountain.

A curdled mountain, a fat mountain. Why suspect ye curdled mountains?

A mountain in which God is well pleased to dwell: for there the Lord shall dwell unto the end.

The chariot of God is attended by ten thousands: thousands of them that rejoice: the Lord is among them in Sinai, in the holy place.

Thou hast ascended on high, Thou hast led captivity captive; Thou hast received gifts in men.

Yea for those also that do believe in the dwelling of the Lord God.

Blessed be the Lord day by day: the God of our salvation will make our journey prosperous to us.

Our God is the God of salvation: and of the Lord, of the Lord are the issues from death.

But God shall break the heads of His enemies: the hairy crown of them that walk on in their sins.

The Lord said: I will turn them from Basam, I will turn them into the depth of the sea:

That thy foot may be dipped in the blood of thy enemies; the tongue of thy dogs be red with the same.

They have seen Thy goings, O God, the goings of my God: of my King Who is in His sanctuary.

Princes went before joined with singers, in the midst of young damsels playing on timbrels.

In the churches bless ye God the Lord from the fountains of Israel.

There is Benjamin a youth, in ecstasy of mind.

The princes of Juda are their leaders: the princes of Zabulon, the princes of Nephthali.

Command Thy strength, O God: confirm, O God, what Thou hast wrought in us.

From Thy temple in Jerusalem, kings shall offer presents to Thee.

Rebuke the wild beasts of the reeds, the congregation of bulls with the kine of the people: who seek to exclude them who are tried with silver.

Scatter Thou the nations that delight in wars: ambassadors shall come out of Egypt:

Ethiopia shall soon stretch out her hands to God.

Sing to God, ye kingdoms of the earth: sing ye to the Lord:

Sing ye to God Who mounteth above the heaven of heavens to the east.

Behold He will give to His voice the voice of power; give ye glory to God for Israel, His magnificence, and His power is in the clouds.

God is wonderful in His Saints, the God of Israel is He Who will give power and strength to His People. Blessed be God.

Glory be to the Father, and to the Son, and to the Holy Ghost.

As it was in the beginning, is now, and ever shall be, world without end. Amen.

Antiphon. Confirm, O God, what Thou hast wrought in us: from Thy holy temple which is in Jerusalem. Alleluia. Alleluia.

Antiphon. Send forth Thy spirit, and they shall be created: and Thou shalt renew the face of the earth. Alleluia, Alleluia.

Psalm 103

Bless the Lord, O my soul: O Lord my God. Thou art exceedingly great.

Thou hast put on praise and beauty: and art clothed with light as with a garment.

Who stretchest out the heaven like a pavilion: Who coverest the higher rooms thereof with water.

Who makest the clouds Thy chariot: Who walkest upon the wings of the winds.

Who makest Thy angels spirits: and Thy ministers a burning fire.

Who hast founded the earth on its own bases: it shall not be moved for ever and ever.

The deep like a garment is its clothing: above the mountains shall the waters stand.

At Thy rebuke they shall flee: at the voice of Thy thunder they shall fear.

The mountains ascend, and the plains descend into the place which Thou hast founded for them.

Thou hast set a bound which they shall not pass over: neither shall they return to cover the earth.

Thou sendest forth springs in the vales; between the midst of the hills the waters shall pass.

All the beasts of the field shall drink: the wild asses shall expect in their thirst.

Over them the birds of the air shall dwell: from the midst of the rocks they shall give forth their voices.

Thou waterest the hills from Thy upper rooms: the earth shall be filled with the fruit of Thy works

Bringing forth grass for cattle, and herb for the service of men.

That Thou mayest bring bread out of the earth: and that wine may cheer the heart of man.

That he may make the face cheerful with oil: and that bread may strengthen men's hearts.

The trees of the field shall be filled, and the cedars of Libanus which He hath planted: there the sparrows shall make their nests.

The highest of them is the house of the heron. The high hills are a refuge for the harts, the rock for the urchins.

He hath made the moon for seasons: the sun knoweth his going down.

Thou hast appointed darkness, and it is night: in it shall all the beasts of the woods go about.

The young lions roaring after their prey, and seeking their meat from God.

The sun ariseth, and they are gathered together: and they shall lie down in their dens.

Man shall go forth to his work, and to his labor until the evening.

How great are Thy works, O Lord? Thou hast made all things in wisdom: the earth is filled with Thy riches.

So is this great sea which stretcheth wide its arms: there are creeping things without number.

Creatures little and great. There the ships shall go.

This sea-dragon which Thou hast formed to play therein. All expect of Thee that Thou give them food in season.

What Thou givest to them they shall gather up: when Thou openest Thy hand, they shall all be filled with good.

But if Thou turnest away Thy face, they shall be troubled: Thou shalt take away their breath, and they shall fail, and shall return to their dust.

Thou shalt send forth Thy Spirit; and they shall be created: and Thou shalt renew the face of the earth.

May the glory of the Lord endure for ever: the Lord shall rejoice in His works.

He looketh upon the earth and maketh it tremble: He toucheth the mountains and they smoke.

I will sing to the Lord, as long as I live: I will sing praise to my God while I have my being.

Let my speech be acceptable to Him: but I will take delight in the Lord.

Let sinners be consumed out of the earth, and the unjust, so that they may be no more. O my soul, bless thou the Lord.

Glory be to the Father, and to the Son, and to the Holy Ghost.

As it was in the beginning, is now, and ever shall be, world without end. Amen.

Antiphon. Send forth Thy spirit, and they shall be created: and Thou shalt renew the face of the earth. Alleluia. Alleluia.

V. The Spirit of the Lord hath filled the whole world. Alleluia.

R. And that which containeth all things, hath knowledge of the voice. Alleluia.

Our Father, etc.

V. And lead us not into temptation.

R. But deliver us from evil. Amen.

The Absolution

Graciously hear, O Lord Jesus Christ, the prayers of Thy servants, and have mercy upon us; Who, with the Father and the Holy Ghost, livest and reignest, world without end.

R. Amen.

V. Pray sir, a blessing.

The Blessing

May the lesson of the Gospel be unto us salvation and protection.

R. Amen.

The lesson of the Holy Gospel according to John (ch. 14, v. 23).

First Lesson

At that time: Jesus said to His disciples: If any man love Me, he will keep My word, and My Father will love him, and We will come to him, and will make Our abode with him.

Homily by Pope St. Gregory

(*Homily 30, on the Gospel.*)

Dearly beloved brethren, our best way will be to run briefly through the words which have been read from the Holy Gospel, and thereafter rest for a while quietly gazing upon the solemn subject of this great festival. This is the day whereon "suddenly there came a sound from heaven," and the Holy Ghost descended upon the Apostles, and, for fleshly minds, gave them minds wherein the love of God was shed abroad; and, while without "there appeared unto them cloven tongues, like as of fire, and it sat upon each of them," within their hearts were enkindled. While they received the visible presence of God in the form of fire, the flames of His love enwrapped them. The Holy Ghost Himself is love; whence is that John saith: "God is love." Whosoever therefore loveth God with all his soul, already hath obtained Him Whom he loveth; for no man is able to love God, if he have not gained Him Whom he loveth.

But Thou, O Lord, have mercy on us.

R. Amen.

R. When the days of Pentecost were accomplished, they were all together in one place, Alleluia: and suddenly there came a sound from heaven, Alleluia: as of a mighty wind coming, and it filled the whole house. Alleluia. Alleluia.

V. Whilst, therefore, the disciples were all gathered together in one place for fear of the Jews, there suddenly came upon them a sound from heaven.

R. As of a mighty wind, and it filled the whole house. Alleluia. Alleluia.

V. Pray sir, a blessing.

The Blessing

May the Divine assistance always remain with us.
R. Amen.

Second Lesson

But, behold, now, if I shall ask any one of you whether he loveth God, he will answer with all boldness and quietness of spirit: "I do love Him." But at the very beginning of this day's Lesson from the Gospel, ye have heard what the Truth saith: "If any man love Me, he will keep My word." The test, then, of love, is whether it is showed by works. Hence the same John hath said in his Epistle: "Whoever sayeth, I love God, and keepeth not His commandments, he is a liar." Then do we indeed love God, and keep His commandments, if we deny ourselves the gratification of our appetites. Whosoever still wandereth after unlawful desires, such an one plainly loveth not God, for he saith: nay, to that which God willeth.

But thou, O Lord, have mercy on us.

R. Amen.

R. They were all filled with the Holy Ghost, and they began to speak, according as the Holy Ghost gave them to speak. And the multitude came together saying, Alleluia.

V. The Apostles spoke in divers tongues the wonderful works of God.

R. And the multitude came together saying, Alleluia.

V. Glory be to the Father, and to the Son, and to the Holy Ghost.

R. And the multitude came saying Alleluia.

V. Pray sir, a blessing.

The Blessing

May the King of Angels conduct us to the company of the heavenly citizens.

R. Amen.

Third Lesson

"And My Father will love him, and We will come to him and make Our abode with him." O my dearly beloved brethren, think what a dignity is that, to have God abiding as a guest in our heart! Surely if some rich man or some powerful friend were to come into our house, we would hasten to have our whole house cleaned, lest, perchance, when he came in, he should see aught to displease his eye. So let him that would make his mind an abode for God, cleanse it from all the filth of works of iniquity. Lo, again, what saith the Truth? "We will come to him, and make Our abode with him." There are some hearts whereunto God cometh, but maketh not His abode therein; with a certain pricking, they feel His presence, but in time of temptation, they forget that which hath pricked them: and so they turn again to work unrighteousness, even as though they had never repented.

But thou, O Lord, have mercy on us.

R. Amen.

Te Deum

We praise Thee, O God: we acknowledge Thee to be the Lord.

All the earth doth worship Thee: the Father everlasting.

To Thee all Angels: to Thee the Heavens and all the Powers therein:

To Thee the Cherubim and Seraphim: cry with unceasing voice:

Holy, Holy, Holy: Lord God of Hosts.

The heavens and the earth are full: of the majesty of Thy glory.

Thee the glorious choir: of the Apostles.

Thee the admirable company: of the Prophets.

Thee the white-robed army of martyrs: praise.

Thee the Holy Church throughout all the world: doth acknowledge.

The Father: of infinite Majesty.

Thine adorable, true: and only Son.

Also the Holy Ghost: the Paraclete.

Thou art the King of Glory: O Christ.

Thou art the everlasting Son: of the Father.

Thou having taken upon Thee to deliver man: didst not abhor the Virgin's womb.

Thou having overcome the sting of death: didst open to believers the Kingdom of Heaven.

Thou sittest at the right hand of God: in the glory of the Father.

We believe that Thou shalt come: to be our Judge.

We beseech Thee, therefore, help Thy servants: whom Thou hast redeemed with Thy precious Blood.

Make them to be numbered with Thy Saints: in glory everlasting.

O Lord, save Thy people: and bless Thine inheritance.

Govern them: and lift them up for ever.

Day by day: we bless Thee.

And we praise Thy name for ever: and world without end.

Vouchsafe, O Lord, this day: to keep us without sin.

Have mercy on us, O Lord: have mercy on us.

Let Thy mercy, O Lord, be upon us: as we have hoped in Thee.

O Lord, in Thee have I hoped: let me never be confounded.

Lauds

V. Incline unto mine aid, O God.

R. O Lord, make haste to help me.

Glory be to the Father, and to the Son, and to the Holy Ghost: as it was in the beginning, is now, and ever shall be, world without end. Amen.

Antiphon. When the days of Pentecost were accomplished, they were all together in one place. Alleluia

Psalm 92

The Lord hath reigned, He is clothed with beauty: the Lord is clothed with strength, and hath girded Himself.

For He hath established the world which shall not be moved.

Thy throne is prepared from of old: Thou art from everlasting.

The floods have lifted up, O Lord: the floods have lifted up their voice.

The floods have lifted up their waves, with the noise of many waters.

Wonderful are the surges of the sea: wonderful is the Lord on high.

Thy testimonies are become exceedingly credible: holiness becometh Thy house, O Lord, unto length of days.

Glory be to the Father, and to the Son, and to the Holy Ghost.

As it was in the beginning, is now, and ever shall be, world without end. Amen.

Antiphon. When the days of Pentecost were accomplished, they were all together in one place. Alleluia.

Antiphon. The Spirit of the Lord hath filled the whole world. Alleluia.

Psalm 99

Sing joyfully to God, all the earth: serve ye the Lord with gladness.

Come in before His presence with exceeding great joy.

Know ye that the Lord He is God: He made us and not we ourselves.

We are His people and the sheep of His pasture. Go ye into His gates with praise, into His courts with hymns: and give glory to Him.

Praise ye His name: for the Lord is sweet, His mercy endureth for ever, and His truth to generation and generation.

Glory be to the Father, and to the Son, and to the Holy Ghost.

As it was in the beginning, is now, and ever shall be, world without end. Amen.

Antiphon. The Spirit of the Lord hath filled the whole world. Alleluia.

Antiphon. They were all filled with the Holy Ghost, and they began to speak. Alleluia. Alleluia.

Psalm 62

O God my God, to Thee do I watch at break of day.

For Thee my soul hath thirsted: for Thee my flesh. O how many ways.

In a desert land, and where there is no way, and no water: so in the sanctuary have I come before Thee, to see Thy power and Thy glory.

For Thy mercy is better than lives: Thee my lips shall praise.

Thus will I bless Thee all my life long: and in Thy name I will lift up my hands.

Let my soul be filled as with marrow and fatness: and my mouth shall praise Thee with joyful lips.

If I have remembered Thee, upon my bed, I will meditate on Thee in the morning: because Thou hast been my helper.

And I will rejoice under the covert of Thy wings: my soul hath stuck close to Thee: Thy right hand hath received me.

But they have sought my soul in vain, they shall go into the lower parts of the earth:

They shall be delivered into the hands of the sword, they shall be the portions of foxes.

But the King shall rejoice in God, all they shall be praised that swear by Him: because the mouth is stopped of them that speak wicked things.

Psalm 66

May God have mercy on us and bless us: may He cause the light of His countenance to shine upon us, and may He have mercy on us.

That we may know Thy way upon earth: Thy salvation in all nations.

Let the people confess to Thee, O God, let all the people give praise to Thee.

Let the nations be glad and rejoice: for Thou judgest the people with justice, and directest the nations upon earth.

Let the people, O God, confess to Thee: let all the people give praise to Thee: the earth hath yielded her fruit.

May God, our God bless us, may God bless us; and all the ends of the earth fear Him.

Glory be to the Father, and to the Son, and to the Holy Ghost.

As it was in the beginning, is now, and ever shall be, world without end. Amen.

Antiphon. They were all filled with the Holy Ghost, and they began to speak. Alleluia. Alleluia.

Antiphon. O ye fountains, and all that move in the waters, sing ye a hymn unto God. Alleluia.

Canticle of the Three Children

(Daniel, ch. 3.)

All ye works of the Lord, bless the Lord: praise and exalt Him above all for ever.

O ye Angels of the Lord, bless the Lord: O ye heavens, bless the Lord.

O all ye waters that are above the heavens, bless the Lord: O all ye powers of the Lord, bless the Lord.

O ye sun and moon, bless the Lord: O ye stars of heaven, bless the Lord.

O every shower and dew, bless ye the Lord: O all ye Spirits of God, bless the Lord.

O ye fire and heat, bless the Lord: O ye cold and heat, bless the Lord.

O ye dews and hoarfrosts bless the Lord: O ye frost and cold, bless the Lord.

O ye ice and snow, bless the Lord: O ye nights and days, bless the Lord.

O ye light and darkness, bless the Lord: O ye lightnings and clouds, bless the Lord.

O let the earth bless the Lord: let it praise and exalt Him above all for ever.

O ye mountains and hills, bless the Lord: O all ye things that spring up in the earth, bless the Lord.

O ye fountains, bless the Lord: O ye seas and rivers, bless the Lord.

O ye whales, and all that move in the waters, bless the Lord: O all ye fowls of the air, bless the Lord.

O all ye beasts and cattle, bless the Lord: O ye sons of men, bless the Lord.

O let Israel bless the Lord: let them praise and exalt Him above all for ever.

O ye priests of the Lord, bless the Lord: O ye servants of the Lord, bless the Lord.

O ye spirits and souls of the just, bless the Lord: O ye holy and humble of heart, bless the Lord.

O Ananias, Azarias, and Misael, bless ye the Lord: praise and exalt Him above all for ever.

Let us bless the Father, and the Son, with the Holy Ghost: let us praise and exalt Him above all for ever.

Blessed art Thou, O Lord, in the firmament of heaven: and worthy to be praised and glorified, and exalted above all forever.

Antiphon. O ye fountains, and all that move in the waters, sing ye a hymn unto God. Alleluia.

Antiphon. The Apostles spoke in divers tongues the wonderful works of God. Alleluia. Alleluia. Alleluia.

Psalm 148

Praise ye the Lord from the heavens: praise ye Him in the high places.

Praise ye Him, all His angels: praise ye Him, all His hosts.

Praise ye Him, O sun and moon: praise Him all ye stars and light.

Praise Him, ye heavens of heavens: and let all the

waters that are above the heavens praise the name of the Lord.

For He spake, and they were made: He commanded, and they were created.

He hath established them for ever, and for ages and ages: He hath made a decree, and it shall not pass away.

Praise the Lord from the earth, ye dragons, and all ye deeps.

Fire, hail, snow, ice, stormy winds, which fulfill His words.

Mountains and all hills, fruitful trees, and all cedars.

Beasts and all cattle: serpents and feathered fowls.

Kings of the earth and all people: princes and all judges of the earth.

Young men and maidens: let the old with the younger, praise the name of the Lord, for His name alone is exalted.

The praise of Him is above heaven and earth: and He hath exalted the horn of His people.

A hymn to all His Saints: to the children of Israel, a people approaching to Him.

Psalm 149

Sing ye to the Lord a new canticle: let His praise be in the church of the Saints.

Let Israel rejoice in Him that made him: and let the children of Sion be joyful in their King.

Let them praise His name in choir: let them sing to Him with the timbrel and the psaltery.

For the Lord is well pleased with His people: and He will exalt the meek unto salvation.

The Saints shall rejoice in glory: they shall be joyful in their beds.

The high praises of God shall be in their mouth: and two-edged swords in their hands.

To execute vengeance upon the nations, chastisements among the people:

To bind their Kings with fetters, and their nobles with manacles of iron.

To execute upon them the judgment that is written: this glory is to all His Saints.

Psalm 150

Praise ye the Lord in His holy places: praise ye Him in the firmament of His power.

Praise ye Him for His mighty acts: praise ye Him according to the multitude of His greatness.

Praise Him with sound of trumpet: praise Him with psaltery and harp.

Praise Him with timbrel and choir: praise Him with strings and organs.

Praise Him on high sounding cymbals: praise Him on cymbals of joy: let every spirit praise the Lord.

Glory be to the Father, and to the Son, and to the Holy Ghost.

As it was in the beginning, is now, and ever shall be, world without end. Amen.

Antiphon. The Apostles spoke in divers tongues the wonderful works of God. Alleluia. Alleluia. Alleluia.

The Chapter

(Acts, ch. 2.)

When the days of Pentecost were accomplished, they were all together in one place: and suddenly there came a sound from heaven, as of a mighty wind coming, and it filled the whole house where they were sitting.

R. Thanks be to God.

The Hymn

Round roll the weeks our hearts to greet.
　With blissful joy returning;
For lo! The Holy Paraclete
　On twelve bright brows sits burning:
　　With quivering flame He lights on each,
　　In fashion like a tongue, to teach
　　That eloquent they are of speech.
　Their hearts with true love yearning.
While with all tongues they speak to all
　The nations deem them maddened:

And drunk with wine the Gentiles call,
   Whom God's good Spirit gladdened;
      A marvel this—in mystery done—
      The Holy Paschal-tide outrun
      By numbers told whose reckoning won
   Remission for the saddened,

O God most holy. Thee we pray
   With reverent brow low bending,
Grant us the Spirit's gifts to-day,—
   The gifts from heaven descending.
      And since Thy grace hath deigned to hide
      Within our breasts once sanctified,
      Deign, Lord, to cast our sins aside,
   Henceforth calm seasons sending.

To God the Father, laud and praise.
   Praise to the Son be given;
Praise to the Spirit of all grace,
   The Fount of graces seven—
      As was of old, all worlds before,
      Is now, and shall be evermore
      When time and change are spent and o'er,—
   All praise in earth and heaven. Amen.
   V. They were all filled with the Holy Ghost. Alleluia.
   R. And they began to speak. Alleluia.

Antiphon. Receive ye the Holy Ghost: whose sins you shall forgive, they are forgiven them. Alleluia.

The Canticle of Zachary

(Luke, ch. 1.)

Blessed be the Lord God of Israel: because He hath visited and wrought the redemption of His people:

And hath raised up a horn of salvation to us, in the house of David, His servant.

As He spake by the mouth of His holy prophets, who are from the beginning:

Salvation from our enemies, and from the hand of all that hate us.

To perform mercy to our fathers: and to remember His holy testament.

The oath which He swore to Abraham our Father, that He would grant to us.

That being delivered from the hand of our enemies, we may serve Him without fear,

In holiness and justice before Him, all our days.

And thou child, shalt be called the Prophet of the Highest: for thou shalt go before the face of the Lord, to prepare His ways.

To give knowledge of salvation to His people, unto remission of their sins.

Through the bowels of the mercy of our God, in which the Orient, from on high, hails visited us.

To enlighten them that sit in darkness, and in the shadow of death: to direct our feet into the way of peace.

Glory be to the Father, and to the Son, and to the Holy Ghost.

As it was in the beginning, is now, and ever shall be, world without end. Amen.

Antiphon. Receive ye the Holy Ghost: whose sins you shall forgive, they are forgiven them. Alleluia.

V. O Lord, hear my prayer.

R. And let my cry come unto Thee.

Let us pray:

O God Who, on this day, didst teach the hearts of the faithful, by the light of the Holy Spirit: grant us by the same Spirit to have a right judgment in all things and evermore to rejoice in His holy comfort. Through our Lord Jesus Christ, Thy Son, who liveth and reigneth with Thee, in unity with the same Holy Spirit, one God, world without end.

R. Amen.

V. O Lord, hear my prayer.

R. And let my cry come unto Thee.

V. Let us bless the Lord.

R. Thanks be to God.

V. And may the souls of the faithful, through the mercy of God, rest in peace.

R. Amen.

Our Father, etc.

V. May the Lord give us His peace.

R. And life everlasting. Amen.

Antiphon of the Blessed Virgin Mary

O Queen of Heaven, rejoice! Alleluia.
For He whom thou didst merit to bear—Alleluia.
Hath risen, as He said. Alleluia.
Pray for us to God. Alleluia.
V. Rejoice and be glad, O Virgin Mary. Alleluia.
R. For the Lord hath risen indeed. Alleluia.

Let us pray:

O God, who, through the Resurrection of Thy Son our Lord Jesus Christ, didst vouchsafe to fill the world with joy: grant, we beseech Thee, that through His Virgin Mother, Mary, we may lay hold on the joys of everlasting life. Through the same Christ our Lord.

R. Amen.

V. May the Divine assistance always remain with us.

R. Amen.

4. Prayer after Divine Office

To the Most Holy and undivided Trinity, to the Humanity of our Lord Jesus Christ crucified, to the faithful Virginity of the most blessed and most glorious Mary, ever Virgin, and to the whole company of the Saints, be everlasting praise, honor, and glory, by all creatures; and to us remission of all our sins, world without end. Amen.

V. Blessed be the womb of the Virgin Mary, which bore the Son of the Eternal Father.

R. And blessed be the breasts which nourished Christ the Lord.

Our Father. Hail Mary.

5. Prime

Our Father. Hail Mary. I believe.

V. Incline unto mine aid, O God.

R. O Lord, make haste to help me.

Glory be to the Father, and to the Son, and to the Holy Ghost: as it was in the beginning, is now, and ever shall be, world without end. Amen. Alleluia.

The Hymn

The star of morn to night succeeds;
    We therefore meekly pray,
May God, in all our words and deeds,
    Keep us from harm this day.

May He in love restrain us still
From tones of strife and words of ill,
And wrap around and close our eyes
To earth's absorbing vanities.

May wrath and thoughts that gender shame
    Ne'er in our breasts abide,
And painful abstinences tame
    Of wanton flesh the pride.

So when the weary day is o'er,
And night and stillness come once more,
Blameless and clean from spot of earth
We may repeat with reverent mirth—

To God the Father, and the Son
    Who rose from death, be glory given,
With Thee, O holy Comforter,
      Henceforth by all in earth and heaven.
                    Amen.

Antiphon. When the days of Pentecost were accomplished.

Psalm 53

Save me, O God, by Thy name, and judge me in Thy strength.

O God, hear my prayer: give ear to the words of my mouth.

For strangers have risen up against me; and the mighty have sought after my soul: and they have not set God before their eyes.

For behold God is my helper: and the Lord is the protector of my soul.

Turn back the evils upon my enemies: and cut them off in Thy truth.

I will freely sacrifice to Thee, and will give praise, O God, to Thy name: because it is good.

For Thou hast delivered me out of all trouble: and my eye hath looked down upon my enemies.

Glory be to the Father, and to the Son, and to the Holy Ghost.

As it was in the beginning, is now, and ever shall be, world without end. Amen.

Psalm 118

Blessed are the undefiled in the way, who walk in the law of the Lord.

Blessed are they that search His testimonies: that seek Him with their whole heart.

For they that work iniquity, have not walked in His ways.

Thou hast commanded Thy commandments to be kept most diligently.

O that my ways may be directed to keep Thy justifications!

Then shall I not be confounded, when I shall look into all Thy commandments.

I will praise Thee with uprightness of heart, when I shall have learned the judgments of Thy justice.

I will keep Thy justifications: O do Thou not utterly forsake me!

By what doth a young man correct his way? by observing Thy words.

With my whole heart have I sought after Thee: let me not stray from Thy commandments.

Thy words have I hidden in my heart, that I may not sin against Thee.

Blessed art Thou, O Lord: teach me Thy justifications.

With my lips I have pronounced all the judgments of Thy mouth.

I have been delighted in the way of Thy testimonies, as in all riches.

I will meditate on Thy commandments: and I will consider Thy ways.

I will think of Thy justifications: I will not forget Thy words.

Glory be to the Father, and to the Son, and to the Holy Ghost.

As it was in the beginning, is now, and ever shall be, world without end. Amen.

Give bountifully to Thy servant, enliven me: and I shall keep Thy words.

Open Thou my eyes: and I will consider the wondrous things of Thy law.

I am a sojourner on the earth: hide not Thy commandments from me.

My soul hath coveted too long for Thy justifications, at all times.

Thou hast rebuked the proud: they are cursed who decline from Thy commandments.

Remove from me reproach and contempt: because I have sought after Thy testimonies.

For princes sat, and spoke against me; but Thy servant was employed in Thy justifications.

For Thy testimonies are my meditation: and Thy justifications my counsel.

My soul hath cleaved to the pavement: quicken Thou me according to Thy word.

I have declared my ways and Thou hast heard me: teach me Thy justifications.

Make me to understand the way of Thy justifications: and I shall be exercised in Thy wondrous works.

My soul hath slumbered through heaviness: strengthen Thou me in Thy words.

Remove from me the way of iniquity: and out of Thy law have mercy on me.

I have chosen the way of truth: Thy judgments I have not forgotten.

I have stuck to Thy testimonies, O Lord: put me not to shame.

I have run the way of Thy commandments, when Thou didst enlarge my heart.

Glory be to the Father, and to the Son, and to the Holy Ghost.

As it was in the beginning, is now, and ever shall be, world without end. Amen.

Antiphon. When the days of Pentecost were accomplished, they were all together in one place.

The Chapter

(1. Tim., ch. 1.)

Unto the King of Ages, the Immortal, Invisible, only God, be honor and glory for ever and ever. Amen.

R. Thanks be to God.

The Short Responsory

Christ, Thou Son of the living God, have mercy on us. Alleluia. Alleluia.

Christ, Thou Son of the living God, have mercy on us. Alleluia. Alleluia.

V. Thou that sittest at the right hand of the Father.

R. Alleluia. Alleluia.

V. Glory be to the Father, and to the Son, and to the Holy Ghost.

R. Christ, Thou Son of the living God, have mercy on us. Alleluia. Alleluia.

V. Arise, O Christ and help us. Alleluia.

R. And deliver us for Thy name's sake. Alleluia.

V. O Lord, hear my prayer.

R. And let my cry come unto Thee.

Let us pray:

O Lord, God Almighty, who hast brought us to the beginning of this day: let Thy power so defend us therein, that this day we may fall into no sin, but that all our thoughts, words and works may always tend to what is just in Thy sight. Through our Lord Jesus Christ, Thy Son, who liveth and reigneth with Thee in the unity of the Holy Ghost, one God, world without end. Amen.

V. O Lord, hear my prayer.

R. And let my cry come unto Thee.

V. Let us bless the Lord.

R. Thanks be to God.

V. Precious in the sight of the Lord.

R. Is the death of His Saints.

May the Blessed Virgin Mary and all the Saints plead for us with the Lord that we may deserve to be helped and delivered by Him who liveth and reigneth, world without end. Amen.

V. Incline unto mine aid, O God.

R. O Lord, make haste to help me.

V. Incline unto mine aid, O God.

R. O Lord, make haste to help me.

V. Incline unto mine aid, O God,

R. O Lord, make haste to help me.

V. Glory be to the Father, and to the Son, and to the Holy Ghost.

R. As it was in the beginning, is now, and ever shall be, world without end. Amen.

Our Father.

V. And lead us not into temptation.

R. But deliver us from evil.

V. Look upon Thy servants, O Lord, and upon Thy works, and direct their children.

R. And let the brightness of the Lord our God be upon us, and direct Thou the works of our hands over us: yea, the work of our hands do Thou direct.

V. Glory be to the Father, and to the Son, and to the Holy Ghost.

R. As it was in the beginning, is now, and ever shall be, world without end. Amen.

Let us pray:

O Lord God, King of heaven and earth, vouchsafe this day to direct and to sanctify, to rule and to govern, our souls and bodies, our senses, words, and actions, in Thy law, and in the works of Thy commandments; that both now and forever we may deserve to be saved and delivered through Thy protection, O Savior of the world, who livest and reignest, world without end.

R. Amen.

V. Pray, sir, a blessing.

The Blessing

May the Lord Almighty order our days and deeds in His peace.

R. Amen.

The Short Lesson

(Acts, ch. 2.)

Jews also and proselytes, Cretes and Arabians: We have heard them speak in our own tongues the wonderful works of God.

But thou, O Lord, have mercy on us.

R. Thanks be to God.

V. Our help is in the name of the Lord.

R. Who hath made heaven and earth.

V. Bless ye.

R. God bless us.

The Blessing

The Lord bless us, and keep us from all evil, and bring us unto life everlasting; and may the souls of the faithful, through the mercy of God, rest in peace.

R. Amen.

6. Terce

Our Father. Hail Mary.

V. Incline unto mine aid, O God.

R. O Lord, make haste to help me.

Glory be to the Father, and to the Son, and to the Holy Ghost: as it was in the beginning, is now, and ever shall be, world without end. Amen. Alleluia.

The Hymn

Come, Holy Ghost, Creator, come,
    From Thy bright heavenly throne!
Come take possession of our souls,
    And make them all Thine own!

Thou who art called the Paraclete,
    Best gift of God above,
The Living Spring, the Living Fire,
    Sweet Unction and True Love!

Thou who art sevenfold in Thy grace,
    Finger of God's right hand,
His promise, teaching little ones
    To speak and understand!

O guide our minds with Thy blest light,
    With love our hearts inflame,
And with Thy strength, which ne'er decays,
    Confirm our mortal frame!

Far from us drive our hellish foe,
    True peace unto us bring,
And through all perils guide us safe
    Beneath Thy sacred wing.

Through Thee may we the Father know,
Through Thee the Eternal Son,
And Thee the Spirit of them both
Thrice-blessed Three in One.

Now to the Father, and the Son
Who rose from death, be glory given,
With Thee, the Holy Comforter,
Henceforth by all in earth and heaven.
Amen.

Antiphon. The spirit of the Lord.

Psalm 118

(Continued.)

Set before me for a law the way of Thy justifications, O Lord: and I will always seek after it.

Give me understanding, and I will search Thy law: and I will keep it with my whole heart.

Lead me into the path of Thy commandments: for this same I have desired.

Incline my heart into Thy testimonies, and not to covetousness.

Turn away mine eyes, that they may not behold vanity: quicken me in Thy way.

Establish Thy word to Thy servant, in Thy fear.

Turn away my reproach which I have apprehended: for Thy judgments are delightful.

Behold I have longed after Thy precepts: quicken me in Thy justice.

Let Thy mercy also come upon me, O Lord: Thy salvation according to Thy word.

So shall I answer them that reproach me in anything: that I have trusted in Thy words.

And take not Thou the word of truth utterly out of my mouth: for in Thy words, I have hoped exceedingly.

So shall I always keep Thy law, for ever and ever.

And I walked at large: because I have sought after Thy commandments.

And I spoke of Thy testimonies before kings: and I was not ashamed.

I meditated also on Thy commandments, which I loved.

And I lifted up my hands to Thy commandments, which I loved: and I was exercised in Thy justification.

Glory be to the Father, and to the Son, and to the Holy Ghost.

As it was in the beginning, is now, and ever shall be, world without end. Amen.

Be Thou mindful of Thy word to Thy servant, in which Thou hast given me hope.

This hath comforted me in my humiliation: because Thy word hath enlivened me.

The proud did iniquitously altogether: but I declined not from Thy law.

I remembered, O Lord, Thy judgments of old: and I was comforted.

A fainting hath taken hold of me, because of the wicked that forsake Thy law.

Thy justifications were the subject of my song, in the place of my pilgrimage.

In the night I have remembered Thy name, O Lord: and have kept Thy law.

This happened to me: because I sought after Thy justifications.

O Lord, my portion, I have said: I would keep Thy law.

I entreated Thy face with all my heart: have mercy on me according to Thy word.

I have thought on my ways: and turned my feet unto Thy testimonies.

I am ready and am not troubled: that I may keep Thy commandments.

The cords of the wicked have encompassed me: but I have not forgotten Thy law.

I rose at midnight to give praise to Thee, for the judgments of Thy justification.

I am a partaker with all them that fear Thee, and that keep Thy commandments.

The earth, O Lord, is full of Thy mercy: teach me Thy justifications.

Glory be to the Father, and to the Son, and to the Holy Ghost.

As it was in the beginning, is now, and ever shall be, world without end. Amen.

Thou hast done well with Thy servant, O Lord, according to Thy word.

Teach me goodness and discipline and knowledge: for I have believed Thy commandments.

Before I was humbled I offended: therefore have I kept Thy word.

Thou art good: and in Thy goodness teach me Thy justifications.

The iniquity of the proud hath been multiplied over me: but I will seek Thy commandments with my whole heart.

Their heart is curdled like milk; but I have meditated on Thy law.

It is good for me that Thou hast humbled me, that I may learn Thy justifications.

The law of Thy mouth is good to me, above thousands of gold and silver.

Thy hands have made me and formed me: give me understanding, and I will learn Thy commandments.

They that fear Thee shall see me, and shall be glad: because I have greatly hoped in Thy words.

I know, O Lord, that Thy judgments are equity: and in Thy truth Thou hast humbled me.

O let Thy mercy be for my comfort, according to Thy word unto Thy servant!

Let Thy tender mercies come unto me, and I shall live: for Thy law is my meditation.

Let the proud be ashamed, because they have done unjustly towards me: but I will be employed in Thy commandments.

Let them that fear Thee turn to me: and they that know Thy testimonies.

Let my heart be undefiled in Thy justifications, that I may not be confounded.

Glory be to the Father, and to the Son, and to the Holy Ghost.

As it was in the beginning, is now, and ever shall be, world without end. Amen.

Antiphon. The Spirit of the Lord hath filled the whole world. Alleluia.

The Chapter

(Acts, ch. 2.)

When the days of Pentecost were accomplished, they were all together in one place: and suddenly there came a sound from heaven, as of a mighty wind coming, and it filled the whole house where they were sitting.

V. Thanks be to God.

Short Responsory

The Spirit of the Lord hath filled the whole world. Alleluia. Alleluia.

The Spirit of the Lord hath filled the whole world. Alleluia. Alleluia.

V. And that which containeth all things, hath knowledge of the voice.

R. Alleluia. Alleluia.

V. Glory be to the Father, and to the Son, and to the Holy Ghost.

R. The Spirit of the Lord hath filled the whole world. Alleluia. Alleluia.

V. The Holy Ghost, the Paraclete—Alleluia.

R. He will teach you all things. Alleluia.

V. O Lord, hear my prayer.

R. And let my cry come unto Thee.

Let us pray:

O God, who, on this day, didst teach the hearts of the faithful, by the light of the Holy Spirit: grant us, by the same Spirit, to have a right judgment in all things and evermore to rejoice in His holy comfort: through our Lord Jesus Christ, Thy Son, who liveth and reigneth with Thee in unity with the same Holy Spirit, one God, world without end.

R. Amen.

V. O Lord, hear my prayer.

R. And let my cry come unto Thee.

V. Let us bless the Lord.

R. Thanks be to God.

V. And may the souls of the faithful, through the mercy of God, rest in peace.

R. Amen.

7. Sext

Our Father. Hail Mary.

V. Incline unto mine aid, O God.

R. O Lord, make haste to help me.

Glory be to the Father, and to the Son, and to the Holy Ghost: as it was in the beginning, is now, and ever shall be, world without end. Amen. Alleluia.

The Hymn

God of all truth, and Lord of might,
Who orderest time and change aright,
Sending the early morning ray,
Lighting the glow of perfect day:

Extinguish Thou each sinful fire,
And banish every ill desire:
Confer upon the body health,
And on the heart peace, past all wealth.

Now to the Father, and the Son
Who rose from death, be glory given.
With Thee, the holy Comforter,
Henceforth by all in earth and heaven.

Amen.

Antiphon. They were all filled with the Holy Ghost.

Psalm 118

(Continued.)

My soul hath fainted after Thy salvation: and in Thy word I have very much hoped.

My eyes have failed for Thy word, saying: When wilt Thou comfort me?

For I am become like a bottle in the frost: I have not forgotten Thy justifications.

How many are the days of Thy servant: when wilt Thou execute judgment on them that persecute me!

The wicked have told me fables: but not as Thy law.

All Thy statutes are truth: they have persecuted me unjustly, do Thou help me.

They have almost made an end of me upon earth; but I have not forsaken Thy commandments.

Quicken Thou me according to Thy mercy: and I shall keep the testimonies of Thy mouth.

For ever, O Lord, Thy word standeth firm in heaven.

Thy truth unto all generations: Thou hast founded the earth, and it continueth.

By Thy ordinance the day goeth on: for all things serve Thee.

Unless that Thy law is my meditation, I had then perhaps perished in my abjection.

Thy justifications I will never forget: for by them Thou hast given me life.

I am Thine, save Thou me: for I have sought Thy justifications.

The wicked have waited for me to destroy me: but I have understood Thy testimonies.

I have seen an end of all perfection: Thy commandment is exceeding broad.

Glory be to the Father, and to the Son, and to the Holy Ghost.

As it was in the beginning, is now, and ever shall be, world without end. Amen.

O how have I loved Thy law, O Lord! it is my meditation all the day.

Through Thy commandment, thou hast made me wiser than my enemies: for it is ever with me.

I have understood more than all my teachers: because Thy testimonies are my meditation.

I have had understanding above ancients: because I have sought Thy commandments.

I have restrained my feet from every evil way: that I may keep Thy words.

I have not declined from Thy judgments, because Thou hast set me a law.

How sweet are Thy words to my palate! more than honey to my mouth.

By Thy commandments I have had understanding: therefore have I hated every way of iniquity.

Thy word is a lamp to my feet, and a light to my paths.

I have sworn and am determined to keep, the judgments of Thy justice.

I have been humbled, O Lord, exceedingly: quicken Thou me according to Thy word.

The free offerings of my mouth make acceptable, O Lord: and teach me Thy judgments.

My soul is continually in my hands: and I have not forgotten Thy law.

Sinners have laid a snare for me: but I have not erred from Thy precepts.

I have purchased Thy testimonies for an inheritance for ever: because they are the joy of my heart.

I have inclined my heart to do Thy justifications for ever, for the reward.

Glory be to the Father, and to the Son, and to the Holy Ghost.

As it was in the beginning, is now, and ever shall be, world without end. Amen.

I have hated the unjust: and have loved Thy law.

Thou art my helper and my protector: and in Thy word I have greatly hoped.

Depart from me, ye malignant: and I will search the commandments of my God.

Uphold me according to Thy word, and I shall live: and let me not be confounded in my expectation.

Help me, and I shall be saved: and I will meditate always on Thy justifications.

Thou hast despised all them that fall off from Thy judgments; for their thought is unjust.

I have accounted all the sinners of the earth prevaricators: therefore have I loved Thy testimonies.

Pierce Thou my flesh with Thy fear: for I am afraid of Thy judgments.

I have done judgment and justice: give me not up to them that slander me.

Uphold Thy servant unto good: let not the proud calumniate me.

My eyes have fainted after Thy salvation: and for the word of Thy justice. Deal with Thy servant according to Thy mercy: and teach me Thy justifications.

I am Thy servant: give me understanding that I may know Thy testimonies.

It is time, O Lord, to do: they have dissipated Thy law.

Therefore have I loved Thy commandments above gold and the topaz.

Therefore was I directed to all Thy commandments: I have hated all wicked ways.

Glory be to the Father, and to the Son, and to the Holy Ghost.

As it was in the beginning, is now, and ever shall be, world without end. Amen.

Antiphon. They were all filled with the Holy Ghost, and they began to speak. Alleluia. Alleluia.

The Chapter

(Acts, ch. 27.)

And when this was noised abroad, the multitude came together, and were confounded in mind, because that every man heard them speak in his own tongue.

R. Thanks be to God.

Short Responsory

The Holy Ghost, the Paraclete: Alleluia. Alleluia.

The Holy Ghost, the Paraclete: Alleluia. Alleluia.

V. He will teach you all things.

R. Alleluia. Alleluia.

V. Glory be to the Father, and to the Son, and to the Holy Ghost.

R. The Holy Ghost, the Paraclete: Alleluia. Alleluia.

V. They were all filled with the Holy Ghost. Alleluia.

R. And they began to speak. Alleluia.

V. O Lord, hear my prayer.

R. And let my cry come unto Thee.

Let us pray:

O God, who, on this day, didst teach the hearts of the faithful, by the light of the Holy Spirit; grant us, by the same Spirit, to have a right judgment in all things, and evermore to rejoice in His holy comfort: Through our Lord Jesus Christ, Thy Son, who liveth and reigneth with Thee in unity with the same Holy Spirit, one God, world without end.

R. Amen.

V. O Lord, hear my prayer.

R. And let my cry come unto Thee.

V. And may the souls of the faithful, through the mercy of God, rest in peace.

R. Amen.

8. None

Our Father. Hail Mary.

V. Incline unto mine aid, O God.

R. O Lord, make haste to help me.

Glory be to the Father, and to the Son, and to the Holy Ghost: as it was in the beginning, is now, and ever shall be, world without end. Amen. Alleluia.

The Hymn

O God, of all things secret force,
Thyself unmoved, all motion's source,
Who from the morn till evening's ray,
Dost through all changes guide the day:

The glorious evening that shall last,
Grant us when this short life is past:
That by a holy death attained,
Eternal glory may be gained.

Now to the Father, and the Son
Who rose from death, be glory given,
With Thee, the holy Comforter,
Henceforth by all in earth and heaven.

Amen.

Antiphon. The Apostles spoke.

Psalm 118

(Continued.)

Thy testimonies are wonderful: therefore my soul hath sought them.

The declaration of Thy words giveth light: and giveth understanding to little ones.

I opened my mouth, and panted: because I longed for Thy commandments.

Look Thou upon me, and have mercy on me, according to the judgment of them that love Thy name.

Direct my steps according to Thy word: and let no iniquity have dominion over me.

Redeem me from the calumnies of men: that I may keep Thy commandments.

Make Thy face to shine upon Thy servant: and teach me Thy justifications.

My eyes have sent forth springs of water: because they have not kept Thy law.

Thou art just, O Lord: and Thy judgment is right.

Thou hast commanded justice Thy testimonies: and Thy truth exceedingly.

My zeal hath made me pine away: because my enemies forgot Thy words.

Thy word is exceedingly refined: and Thy servant hath loved it.

I am very young and despised; but I forgot not Thy justifications.

Thy justice is justice for ever: and Thy law is the truth.

Trouble and anguish have found me: Thy commandments are my meditation.

Thy testimonies are justice for ever: give me understanding, and I shall live.

Glory be to the Father, and to the Son, and to the Holy Ghost.

As it was in the beginning, is now, and ever shall be, world without end. Amen.

I cried with my whole heart, hear me, O Lord: I will seek Thy justifications.

I cried unto Thee, save me: that I may keep Thy commandments.

I prevented the dawning of the day, and cried: because in Thy words I very much hoped.

My eyes to Thee have prevented the morning: that I might meditate on Thy words.

Hear Thou my voice, O Lord, according to Thy mercy: and quicken me according to Thy judgment.

They that persecute me have drawn nigh to iniquity; but they are gone far off from Thy law.

Thou art near, O Lord: and all Thy ways are truth.

I have known from the beginning concerning Thy testimonies: that Thou hast founded them for ever.

See my humiliation, and deliver me: for I have not forgotten Thy law:

Judge my judgment, and redeem me: quicken Thou me for Thy word's sake.

Salvation is far from sinners; because they have not sought Thy justifications.

Many, O Lord, are Thy mercies: quicken me according to Thy judgment.

Many are they that persecute me, and afflict me: but I have not declined from Thy testimonies.

I beheld the transgressors, and I pined away: because they kept not Thy word.

Behold I have loved Thy commandments, O Lord: quicken me Thou in Thy mercy.

The beginning of Thy words is truth: all the judgments of Thy justice are for ever.

Glory be to the Father, and to the Son, and to the Holy Ghost.

As it was in the beginning, is now, and ever shall be, world without end. Amen.

Princes have persecuted me without cause: and my heart hath been in awe of Thy words.

I will rejoice at Thy words, as one that hath found great spoil.

I have hated and abhorred iniquity; but I have loved Thy law.

Seven times a day I have given praise to Thee, for the judgments of Thy justice.

Much peace have they that love Thy law, and to them there is no stumbling-block.

I look for Thy salvation, O Lord, and I loved Thy commandments.

My soul hath kept Thy testimonies, and hath loved them exceedingly.

I have kept Thy commandments and Thy testimonies: because all my ways are in Thy sight.

Let my supplication, O Lord, come near in Thy sight: give me understanding according to Thy word.

Let my request come in before Thee: deliver Thou me according to Thy word.

My lips shall utter a hymn, when Thou shalt teach me Thy justifications.

My tongue shall pronounce Thy word: because all Thy commandments are justice.

Let Thy hand be with me to save me; for I have chosen Thy precepts.

I have longed for Thy salvation, O Lord: and Thy law is my meditation.

My soul shall live and shall praise Thee: and Thy judgments shall help me.

I have gone astray like a sheep that is lost: seek Thy servant, because I have not forgotten Thy commandments.

Glory be to the Father, and to the Son, and to the Holy Ghost.

As it was in the beginning, is now, and ever shall be, world without end. Amen.

Antiphon. The Apostles spoke in divers tongues the wonderful works of God. Alleluia. Alleluia. Alleluia.

The Chapter

(Acts, ch. 2.)

Jews also and proselytes, Cretes and Arabians: we have heard them speak in our own tongues the wonderful works of God.

R. Thanks be to God.

The Short Responsory

They were all filled with the Holy Ghost. Alleluia. Alleluia.

They were all filled with the Holy Ghost. Alleluia. Alleluia.

V.　And they began to speak.

R.　Alleluia. Alleluia.

V.　Glory be to the Father, and to the Son, and to the Holy Ghost.

R.　They were all filled with the Holy Ghost. Alleluia. Alleluia.

V.　The Apostles spoke in divers tongues. Alleluia.

R.　The wonderful works of God. Alleluia.

V.　O Lord, hear my prayer.

R.　And let my cry come unto Thee.

Let us pray:

O God, who, this day, didst teach the hearts of the faithful, by the light of the Holy Spirit: grant us, by the same Spirit, to have a right judgment in all things, and evermore to rejoice in His holy comfort: Through our Lord Jesus Christ, Thy Son, who liveth and reigneth, with Thee in the unity of the same Holy Spirit, one God, world without end.

R.　Amen.

V.　O Lord, hear my prayer.

R. And let my cry come unto Thee.

V. Let us bless the Lord.

R. Thanks be to God.

V. And may the souls of the faithful, through the mercy of God, rest in peace.

R. Amen.

9. Vespers

Our Father. Hail Mary.

V. Incline unto mine aid, O God.

R. O Lord, make haste to help me.

Glory be to the Father, and to the Son, and to the Holy Ghost: as it was in the beginning, is now, and ever shall be, world without end. Amen. Alleluia.

Antiphon. When the days of Pentecost were accomplished, they were all together in one place. Alleluia.

Psalm 109

The Lord said to my Lord: Sit Thou at my right hand: Until I make Thy enemies Thy footstool.

The Lord will send forth the scepter of Thy power out of Sion: rule Thou in the midst of Thy enemies.

With Thee is the principality in the day of Thy strength: in the brightness of the saints: from the womb before the daystar I begot Thee.

The Lord hath sworn, and He will not repent:

Thou art a priest for ever according to the order of Melchisedec.

The Lord at Thy right hand hath broken kings in the day of His wrath.

He shall judge among nations, He shall fill ruins: He shall crush the heads in the land of many.

He shall drink of the torrent in the way: therefore shall He lift up the head.

Glory be to the Father, and to the Son, and to the Holy Ghost.

As it was in the beginning, is now, and ever shall be, world without end. Amen.

Antiphon. When the days of Pentecost were accomplished, they were all together in one place. Alleluia.

Antiphon. The Spirit of the Lord hath filled the whole world. Alleluia.

Psalm 110

I will praise Thee, O Lord, with my whole heart, in the council of the just, and in the congregation.

Great are the works of the Lord: sought out according to all His wills.

His work is praise and magnificence: and His justice continueth for ever and ever.

He hath made a remembrance of His wonderful works, being a merciful and gracious Lord: He hath given food to them that fear Him.

He will be mindful for ever of His covenant: he will show forth to His people the power of His works.

That He may give them the inheritance of the Gentiles: the works of His hands are truth and judgment.

All His commandments are faithful: confirmed for ever and ever, made in truth and equity.

He hath sent redemption to His people: He hath commanded His covenant for ever.

Holy and terrible is His name: the fear of the Lord is the beginning of wisdom.

A good understanding to all that do it: His praise continueth for ever and ever.

Glory be to the Father, and to the Son, and to the Holy Ghost.

As it was in the beginning, is now, and ever shall be, world without end. Amen.

Antiphon. The Spirit of the Lord hath filled the whole world. Alleluia.

Antiphon. They were all filled with the Holy Ghost, and they began to speak. Alleluia. Alleluia.

Psalm 111

Blessed is the man that feareth the Lord: he shall delight exceedingly in His commandments.

His seed shall be mighty upon earth: the generation of the righteous shall be blessed.

Glory and wealth shall be in his house: and his justice remaineth for ever and ever.

To the righteous a light is risen up in darkness: He is merciful, and compassionate and just.

Acceptable is the man that showeth mercy and lendeth; he shall order his words with judgment: because he shall not be moved for ever.

The just shall be in everlasting remembrance: he shall not fear the evil hearing.

His heart is ready to hope in the Lord: his heart is strengthened, he shall not be moved, until he look over his enemies.

He hath distributed, He hath given to the poor: His justice remaineth for ever and ever: his horn shall be exalted in glory.

The wicked shall see, and shall be angry, he shall gnash with his teeth and pine away: the desire of the wicked shall perish.

Glory be to the Father, and to the Son, and to the Holy Ghost.

As it was in the beginning, is now, and ever shall be, world without end. Amen.

Antiphon. They were all filled with the Holy Ghost, and they began to speak. Alleluia. Alleluia.

Antiphon. O ye fountains, and all that move in the waters, sing ye a hymn unto God. Alleluia.

Psalm 112

Praise the Lord, ye children: praise ye the name of the Lord.

Blessed be the name of the Lord, from henceforth now and for ever.

From the rising of the sun unto the going down of the same, the name of the Lord is worthy of praise.

The Lord is high above all nations: and His glory above the heavens.

Who is as the Lord our God, Who dwelleth on high: and looketh down on the low things in heaven and in earth?

Raising up the needy from the earth, and lifting up the poor out of the dunghill.

That He may place him with princes, with the princes of His people.

Who maketh a barren woman to dwell in a house, the joyful mother of children.

Glory be to the Father, and to the Son, and to the Holy Ghost.

As it was in the beginning, is now, and ever shall be, world without end. Amen.

Antiphon. O ye fountains, and all that move in the waters, sing ye a hymn unto God. Alleluia.

Antiphon. The Apostles spoke in divers tongues the wonderful works of God. Alleluia. Alleluia. Alleluia.

Psalm 113

When Israel went out of Egypt, the house of Jacob from a barbarous people.

Judea was made His sanctuary, Israel His dominion.

The sea saw and fled: Jordan was turned back.

The mountains skipped like rams, and the hills like the lambs of the flock.

What ailed thee, O thou sea, that thou didst flee: and thou, O Jordan, that thou wast turned back?

Ye mountains, that ye skipped like rams, and ye hills like lambs of the flock?

At the presence of the Lord the earth was moved, at the presence of the God of Jacob.

Who turned the rocks into pools of water, and the stony hill into fountains of waters.

Not to us, O Lord, not to us; but to Thy name give glory.

For Thy mercy, and for Thy truth's sake: lest the Gentiles should say: Where is their God?

But our God is in heaven: He hath done all things whatsoever he would.

The idols of the Gentiles are silver and gold: the works of the hands of men.

They have mouths and speak not: they have eyes and see not.

They have ears and hear not: they have noses and smell not.

They have hands and feel not: they have feet and walk not: neither shall they cry out through their throat.

Let them that make them become like unto them: and all such as trust in them.

The house of Israel hath hoped in the Lord: He is their helper and their protector.

The house of Aaron hath hoped in the Lord: He is their helper and their protector.

They that fear the Lord have hoped in the Lord: He is their helper and their protector.

The Lord hath been mindful of us, and hath blessed us.

He hath blessed the house of Israel: He hath blessed the house of Aaron.

He hath blessed all that fear the Lord, both little and great.

May the Lord add blessings upon you: upon you and your children.

Blessed be you of the Lord, Who made heaven and earth.

The heaven of heaven is the Lord's: but the earth He has given to the children of men.

The dead shall not praise Thee, O Lord: nor any of them that go down to hell.

But we that live bless the Lord: from this time now and for ever.

Glory be to the Father, and to the Son, and to the Holy Ghost.

As it was in the beginning, is now, and ever shall be, world without end. Amen.

Antiphon. The Apostles spoke in divers tongues the wonderful works of God. Alleluia. Alleluia. Alleluia.

The Chapter

(Acts, ch. 2.)

When the days of Pentecost were accomplished, they were all together in one place; and suddenly there came a sound from heaven, as of a mighty wind coming, and it filled the whole house where they were sitting.

R. Thanks be to God.

The Hymn

Come, Holy Ghost, Creator, come,
From Thy bright heavenly throne!
Come, take possession of our souls,
And make them all Thine own

Thou who art called the Paraclete,
Best gift of God above,
The Living Spring, the Living Fire,
Sweet Unction and True Love!

Thou Who art sevenfold in Thy grace,
Finger of God's right hand,
His promise, teaching little ones
To speak and understand!

O guide our minds with Thy blest light,
    With love our hearts inflame,
And with Thy strength which ne'er decays
    Confirm our mortal frame!

Far from us drive our hellish foe,
    True peace unto us bring,
And through all perils guide us safe
    Beneath Thy sacred wing.

Through Thee may we the Father know,
    Through Thee the Eternal Son,
And Thee the Spirit of them both,
    Thrice-blessed Three in One.

Now to the Father, and the Son
    Who rose from death, be glory given,
With Thee, the holy Comforter,
    Henceforth by all in earth and heaven.
                            Amen.

V. The Apostles spoke in divers tongues. Alleluia.
R. The wonderful works of God. Alleluia.

Antiphon. On this day, the days of Pentecost were accomplished. Alleluia. On this day the Holy Ghost appeared to the disciples under the form of fire and bestowed upon them His gifts: He sent them forth into all the world to preach and to testify: He that believeth and is baptized, shall be saved. Alleluia.

The Canticle of the Blessed Virgin

(Luke, ch. 1.)

My soul doth magnify the Lord:

And my spirit hath rejoiced in God my Savior.

Because He hath regarded the humility of His hand-maid: for behold from henceforth all generations shall call me blessed.

Because He that is mighty hath done great things to me: and holy is His name.

And His mercy is from generation unto generation to them that fear Him.

He hath shewed might in His arm: He hath scattered the proud in the conceit of their heart.

He hath put down the mighty from their seat, and hath exalted the humble.

He hath filled the hungry with good things: and the rich He hath sent empty away.

He hath received Israel: His servant, being mindful of His mercy.

As He spoke to our fathers, to Abraham and to his seed for ever.

Glory be to the Father, and to the Son, and to the Holy Ghost.

As it was in the beginning, is now, and ever shall be, world without end. Amen.

Antiphon. On this day, the days of Pentecost were

accomplished. Alleluia. On this day, the Holy Ghost appeared to the Apostles under the form of fire and bestowed upon them His gifts: He sent them forth into all the world to preach and to testify: He that believeth and is baptized shall be saved. Alleluia.

V. O Lord, hear my prayer.

R. And let my cry come unto Thee.

Let us pray:

O God, who, on this day, didst teach the hearts of the faithful, by the light of the Holy Spirit: grant us, by the same Spirit, to have a right judgment in all things and evermore to rejoice in His holy comfort: through our Lord Jesus Christ, Thy Son, who liveth and reigneth with Thee in unity with the same Divine Spirit, one God, world without end.

R. Amen.

V. O Lord, hear my prayer

R. And let my cry come unto Thee.

V. Let us bless the Lord.

R. Thanks be to God.

V. And may the souls of the faithful, through the mercy of God, rest in peace.

R. Amen.

Our Father.

V. May the Lord give us His peace.

R. And life everlasting. Amen.

Antiphon of the Blessed Virgin Mary

O Queen of Heaven, rejoice! Alleluia.
For He whom thou didst merit to bear. Alleluia.
Hath arisen as He said. Alleluia.
Pray for us to God. Alleluia.
V. Rejoice and be glad, O Virgin Mary. Alleluia.
R. For the Lord hath risen indeed. Alleluia.

Let us pray:

O God Who through the Resurrection of Thy Son our Lord Jesus Christ, didst vouchsafe to fill the world with joy; grant, we beseech Thee, that, through His Virgin Mother, Mary, we may lay hold on the joys of everlasting life. Through the same Jesus Christ our Lord.

R. Amen.
V. May the Divine assistance always remain with us.
R. Amen.
Our Father. Hail Mary. I believe.

10. Compline

V. Pray, sir, a blessing.

The Blessing

The Lord Almighty grant us a quiet night, and a perfect end.

R. Amen.

Short Lesson

(1 Peter, ch. 5.)

Brethren, be sober and watch: because your adversary the devil, as a roaring lion, goeth about seeking whom he may devour: whom resist ye, strong in faith.

But Thou, O Lord, have mercy on us.

R. Thanks be to God.

V. Our help is in the name of the Lord.

R. Who hath made heaven and earth.

Our Father.

The Confiteor

I confess to Almighty God, to Blessed Mary, ever Virgin, to blessed Michael the Archangel, to blessed John the Baptist, to the holy Apostles Peter and Paul, and to all the Saints, that I have sinned exceedingly in thought, word, and deed, through my fault, through my fault, through my most grievous fault. Therefore I beseech blessed Mary, ever Virgin, blessed Michael the Archangel, blessed John the Baptist, the holy Apostles Peter and Paul, and all the Saints, to pray to the Lord our God for me.

May Almighty God have mercy upon us, and forgive us our sins, and bring us unto life everlasting.

R. Amen.

May the Almighty and merciful Lord grant us pardon, absolution, and remission of our sins.

R. Amen.

V. Convert us, O God, our Savior.

R. And turn away Thine anger from us.

V. Incline unto mine aid, O God.

R. O Lord, make haste to help me.

Glory be to the Father, and to the Son, and to the Holy Ghost: as it was in the beginning, is now, and ever shall be, world without end. Amen. Alleluia.

Antiphon. Alleluia.

Psalm 4

When I called upon Him, the God of my justice heard me: when I was in distress. Thou hast enlarged me.

Have mercy on me: and hear my prayer.

O ye sons of men, how long will you be dull of heart? Why do you love vanity, and seek after lying?

Know ye also that the Lord hath made His holy one wonderful: the Lord will hear me when I shall cry unto Him.

Be ye angry, and sin not: the things you say in your hearts be sorry for them upon your beds.

Offer up the sacrifice of justice, and trust in the Lord: many say: who sheweth us good things?

The light of Thy countenance, O Lord, is signed upon us: Thou hast given gladness in my heart.

By the fruit of their corn, their wine, and oil, they are multiplied.

In peace in the self same I will sleep, and I will rest.

For thou, O Lord, singularly hath settled me in hope.

Glory be to the Father, and to the Son, and to the Holy Ghost.

As it was in the beginning, is now, and ever shall be, world without end. Amen.

Psalm 30

In Thee, O Lord, have I hoped, let me never be confounded: deliver me in Thy justice.

Bow down Thy ear to me: make haste to deliver me.

Be Thou unto me a God, a protector, and a house of refuge, to save me.

For Thou art my strength and my refuge: and for Thy name's sake Thou wilt lead me and nourish me.

Thou wilt bring me out of this snare, which they have hidden for me: for Thou art my protector.

Into Thy hands I commend my spirit: thou hast redeemed me, O Lord, the God of truth.

Glory be to the Father, and to the Son, and to the Holy, Ghost.

As it was in the beginning, is now, and ever shall be, world without end. Amen.

Psalm 90

He that dwelleth in the aid of the Most High, shall abide under the protection of the God of Jacob.

He shall say to the Lord: Thou art my protector, and my refuge: my God, in Him will I trust.

For He hath delivered me from the snare of the hunters, and from the sharp word.

He will overshadow thee with His shoulders: and under His wings thou shalt trust.

His truth shall compass thee with a shield: thou shalt not be afraid of the terror of the night.

Of the arrow that flieth in the day; of the business that walketh about in the dark; of invasion, or of the noonday devil.

A thousand shall fall at thy side, and ten thousand at thy right hand; but it shall not come nigh thee.

But thou shalt consider with thy eyes; and shalt see the reward of the wicked.

Because Thou, O Lord, art my hope: thou hast made the Most High thy refuge.

There shall no evil come to thee: nor shall the scourge come near thy dwelling.

For He hath given His angels charge over thee: to keep thee in all thy ways.

In their hands they shall bear thee up; lest thou dash thy foot against a stone.

Thou shalt walk upon the asp and the basilisk: and thou shalt trample under foot the lion and the dragon.

Because he hoped in Me, I will deliver him: I will protect him, because he hath known My name.

He shall cry to Me, and I will hear him: I am with him in tribulation: I will deliver him, and I will glorify him.

I will fill him with length of days: and I will show him My salvation.

Glory be to the Father, and to the Son, and to the Holy Ghost.

As it was in the beginning, is now, and ever shall be, world without end. Amen.

Psalm 133

Behold, now, bless ye the Lord, all ye servants of the Lord.

Who stand in the house of the Lord, in the courts of the house of our God.

In the nights lift up your hands to the holy places, and bless ye the Lord.

May the Lord out of Sion bless thee, He that made heaven and earth.

Glory be to the Father, and to the Son, and to the Holy Ghost.

As it was in the beginning, is now, and ever shall be, world without end. Amen.

Antiphon. Alleluia. Alleluia. Alleluia.

The Hymn

Now with the fast-departing light,
　　Maker of all, we ask of Thee,
Of Thy great mercy, through the night
　　Our guardian and defense to be.

Far off let idle visions fly:
　　No phantoms of the night molest;
Curb Thou our raging enemy,
　　That we in chaste repose may rest.

To God the Father, and the Son.
　　Who rose from death, be glory given.
With Thee, O Holy Comforter,
　　Henceforth by all in earth and heaven.
　　　　　　　　　　　　　　　　　Amen.

The Little Chapter

(Jeremias, ch. 14.)

But Thou, O Lord, art among us, and Thy name is
called upon us: forsake us not, O Lord, our God.

R. Thanks be to God.

Short Responsory

Into Thy hands, O Lord, I commend my spirit.
Alleluia. Alleluia.

Into Thy hands, O Lord, I commend my spirit. Alleluia. Alleluia.

V. Thou hast redeemed us, O Lord God of truth.

R. Alleluia. Alleluia.

V. Glory be to the Father, and to the Son, and to the Holy Ghost.

R. Into Thy hands, O Lord, I commend my spirit. Alleluia. Alleluia.

V. Keep us, O Lord, as the apple of Thine eye. Alleluia.

R. Protect us under the shadow of Thy wings. Alleluia.

Antiphon. Save us, O Lord.

The Canticle of Simeon

(Luke, ch. 2.)

Now Thou dost dismiss Thy servant, O Lord, according to Thy word, in peace:

Because my eyes have seen Thy salvation,

Which Thou hast prepared before the face of all peoples:

A light to the revelation of the Gentiles, and the glory of Thy people Israel.

Glory be to the Father, and to the Son, and to the Holy Ghost.

As it was in the beginning, is now, and ever shall be, world without end. Amen.

Antiphon. Save us, O Lord, waking, and keep us sleeping, that we may watch with Christ, and rest in peace. Alleluia.

V. O Lord, hear my prayer.

R. And let my cry come unto Thee.

Let us pray:

Visit, we beseech Thee, O Lord, this habitation, and drive from it all the snares of the enemy; let Thy holy angels dwell herein, to keep us in peace; and let Thy blessing be upon us for ever. Through our Lord Jesus Christ, Thy Son, who with Thee liveth and reigneth, in unity with the Holy Ghost, one God, world without end.

R. Amen.

V. O Lord, hear my prayer.

R. And let my cry come unto Thee.

V. Let us bless the Lord.

R. Thanks be to God.

The Blessing

May the Almighty and merciful Lord, the Father, the Son, and the Holy Ghost, bless and protect us.

R. Amen.

XIII. Mass of the Holy Ghost for Pentecost Sunday

(From the Roman Missal.)

Introit

(Wisdom, 1:7.)

The Spirit of the Lord hath filled the whole world; and that which containeth all things, hath knowledge of the voice.

Alleluia. Alleluia. Alleluia.

The Collect

O God, Who, on this day, didst teach the hearts of Thy faithful, by the light of the Holy Spirit: grant us, by the same Spirit, to have a right judgment in all things, and evermore to rejoice in His Holy comfort. Through our Lord Jesus Christ, Thy Son, Who liveth and reigneth with Thee in the unity of the same Holy Spirit, one God, world without end. Amen.

Lesson

(Acts 2:1–11.)

When the days of Pentecost were completed, the disciples were all together in one place. And suddenly there came a sound from heaven as of a rushing mighty wind, and it filled the whole house where they were sitting.

And there appeared to them parted tongues as of fire, and it sat upon every one of them: And they were all filled with the Holy Spirit, and began to speak with other tongues, as the Holy Spirit gave them to speak. Now there were dwelling at Jerusalem, Jews, devout men, out of every nation under heaven. And when this voice was spread the multitude came together, and were confounded in mind, because every man heard them speak in his own tongue. And they were all amazed, and wondered, saying: Behold, are not all these who speak Galileans? And how hear we every man our own tongue wherein we were born! Parthians, and Medes, and Elamites, and the inhabitants of Mesopotamia, Judea, and Cappadocia, Pontus, and Asia, Phrygia, and Pamphilia, Egypt, and the parts of Libya about Cyrene, and strangers of Rome, Jews also, and Proselytes, Cretans, and Arabians; we hear them speak in our own tongues the great works of God.

The Gradual

Alleluia. Alleluia.

Send forth Thy Spirit, and they shall be created: and Thou shalt renew the face of the earth. Alleluia.

Come, O Holy Ghost, fill the hearts of Thy faithful and kindle in them the fire of Thy love.

The Sequence

Holy Spirit! Lord of Light!
From Thy clear celestial height
    Thy pure, beaming radiance give.

Come, Thou Father of the poor!
Come, with treasures which endure!
    Come, Thou light of all that live!

Thou, of all consolers, best,
Visiting the troubled breast,
    Dust refreshing peace bestow.

Thou in toil our comfort sweet;
Pleasant coolness in the heat;
    Solace in the midst of woe.

Light immortal! light divine!
Visit Thou these hearts of Thine,
    And our inmost being fill.

If Thou take Thy grace away,
Nothing pure in man will stay;
    All his good is turned to ill.

Heal our wounds—our strength renew;
On our dryness pour Thy dew;
    Wash the stains of guilt away.

Bend the stubborn heart and will;
Melt the frozen, warm the chill;
    Guide the steps that go astray.

Thou on those who evermore
Thee confess and Thee adore
    In Thy sevenfold gifts descend.

Give them comfort when they die;
Give them life with Thee on high;
    Give them joys which never end.
                Amen. Alleluia.

Gospel

(John 14:23–31.)

At that time:—Jesus said to His disciples: If any
one love Me, he will keep My word, and My Father
will love him and We will come to him, and make our
abode with him: he who loveth Me not, keepeth not My
words. And the word which ye have heard, is not Mine,
but the Father's Who sent Me. These things have I spoken to you, abiding with you. But the Paraclete, the
Holy Spirit, Whom the Father will send in My name,
He will teach you all things, and bring all things to your
mind, whatever I have said to you. Peace I leave you,
My peace I give you; not as the world giveth do I give
you. Let not your heart be troubled, nor let it be afraid.
Ye have heard that I said to you: I go away, and I come

to you. If ye loved Me, ye would indeed be glad, because I go to the Father: for the Father is greater than I. And now I have told you before it come to pass, that when it shall come to pass, ye may believe. I will not now speak many things with you: for the prince of this world cometh, and in Me he hath nothing. But that the world may know that I love the Father, and as the Father hath given Me commandment, so do I.

Offertory

(Ps. 67:29–30.)

Confirm, O God, what Thou hast wrought in us: From Thy temple in Jerusalem, kings shall offer presents to Thee. Alleluia.

Secret

Sanctify, we beseech Thee, O Lord, the gifts we have offered to Thee: and cleanse our hearts by the light of the Holy Spirit. Through our Lord Jesus, Thy Son, Who liveth and reigneth with Thee, in unity with the same Holy Ghost, one God, world without end. Amen.

Communion

Suddenly there came a sound from heaven, as of a mighty wind coming, and it filled the whole house where they were sitting. Alleluia.

And they were all filled with the Holy Ghost, speaking the wonderful works of God. Alleluia. Alleluia.

Post Communion

May the infusion of the Holy Spirit cleanse our hearts, O Lord, and render them fruitful by the inward watering of His heavenly dew. Through our Lord Jesus Christ Thy Son, who liveth and reigneth with Thee, in unity with the same Holy Ghost, one God, world without end. Amen.

XIV. The Sacrament of Confirmation

1. Confirmation the completion of the Sacrament of Baptism

In the Sacrament of Baptism the Holy Ghost comes to you for the first time. He then infuses into your soul the life of sanctifying grace, together with Faith, Hope and Charity, and the seed of every other virtue. He then makes you a child of God, and a member of His true Church on earth, and gives you the right to expect all those actual graces you need during the course of your life in order to obtain your everlasting inheritance in heaven.

But you are not always to remain a child. You are to grow up into the fullness of manhood. The life of Divine grace must, therefore, be strengthened and increased within you. Faith, Hope and Charity, and every other virtue must not keep dormant in your soul. They must be reduced to practice and be productive of good fruit. You must ever be a living and active member of God's Church, never be ashamed of your Holy Religion, but ready to profess your Faith openly and willing to lay down your very life in its defense. You must strive to win heaven as a recompense for patient labor and toil performed in God's service, and as a crown of victory gained over the enemies of your soul with whom you have to wrestle until death. You must, in a word, be made a strong and perfect Christian and a valiant soldier of Jesus Christ.

Now all this is done by the Holy Ghost through the Sacrament of Confirmation.

The Sacrament of Confirmation is, therefore, the completion of the Sacrament of Baptism. In Baptism, the Holy Ghost begins the work of your regeneration; in Confirmation, He completes it. And since it is the peculiar work of the Holy Ghost to bring things to their completion and perfection, the Sacrament of Confirmation is the Sacrament of the Holy Ghost in a special manner. In the other Sacraments, the Holy Ghost communicates to your soul His gifts and graces. But, in this Sacrament, He communicates Himself to your soul personally with the fullness of His Divine gifts in order to confirm and complete the work commenced in Baptism. He strengthens and increases within you the life of sanctifying grace so as to enable you to manfully resist all your spiritual enemies. He bestows upon you His sevenfold gift to render the practice of virtue sweet and easy, so that you may abound in merit and good works. He imparts to you in a special manner, courage and strength to practice your Faith in spite of all opposition, and to be determined to lay down your very life rather than swerve from it in the least. He dedicates you as His living temple forever, consecrates you entirely to God's Holy service and enlists you to fight under the banner of Christ. Thus He seals your soul with the indelible mark of a perfect Christian and a true soldier of Jesus Christ.

2. Preparation for the Sacrament of Confirmation

To receive the Sacrament of Confirmation worthily, you must be in the state of grace. It would be a fearful sacrilege to invite the Holy Ghost to enter a soul in which the evil spirit reigns by mortal sin. In addition to this, you must also be animated with the right disposition to derive from this Sacrament all the benefits you can. You must have an earnest longing for the coming of the Holy Ghost into your soul, desirous to give Him full possession over your entire being; and you must be fully determined to live and die as is expected of a perfect Christian and a true soldier of Jesus Christ.

Be persuaded of the necessity and importance of this Divine Sacrament. If anyone wilfully neglects the opportunity of receiving this Sacrament, he is guilty of a grave sin and endangers his eternal salvation.

Remember this Sacrament can be received only once. Hence if you are about to receive it, you must prepare with all possible care. Imitate the example of the Blessed Virgin Mary, the Apostles and the other faithful followers of our Lord, who for nine days prepared themselves for the coming of the Holy Ghost by prayer and retirement. Make a Novena, during which try to spend as much time as you can in thinking of the Power and the Love of the Divine Spirit, and offering up special prayers in His honor. Approach the Sacraments of Confession and Communion. Though they may not be necessary, still nothing could prove a better preparation. The following acts are suggested as an immediate preparation.

An act of Desire. O Divine Spirit, infinite Love of the Father and of the Son, I most earnestly desire that Thou wouldst come to me, and take full possession of my whole being.

Renewal of promises made at Baptism. I now, of my own free will and choice, ratify and renew all the promises made at my Baptism. Come Thou, O Holy Ghost, confirm and complete within me the work commenced by Thee at my Baptism.

An act of Faith. I believe in Thee, God the Holy Ghost, the Lord and Giver of Life, Who proceedest from the Father and the Son; Who together with the Father and the Son art worshipped and glorified; Who didst speak by the Prophets, and Who now speakest by the Catholic Church and, in a special manner, by Thy infallible mouth-piece, the Sovereign Pontiff.

I believe that in this Sacrament of Confirmation, Thou wilt give Thyself to me with the fullness of Thy heavenly gifts in order to make me a perfect Christian and a strong soldier of Jesus Christ.

An act of Hope. Relying on Thine infinite Power and Goodness, I firmly hope that Thou wilt ever assist me in the work of my eternal salvation. I expect, in particular, that, in this Sacrament of Confirmation Thou wilt come to me with the sevenfold gift of Thy holy grace to enable me to fight the good fight and faithfully discharge all the duties of my state in life.

An act of Love. I love Thee, O Divine Spirit, Who art the Eternal Love of the Father and of the Son. I love Thee, O Spirit of infinite Charity, Who hast loved me with an everlasting love. I love Thee, O most tender and compassionate Spirit, Who art my Helper and Protector. I love Thee, O Divine Comforter, Who art about to descend upon me and take up Thy abode within me.

Invitation. O Divine Spirit of infinite Love, Who art sent to me by the Father and by the Son, I invite Thee to come to me and be my soul's sweet Guest. Oh! come and abide with me for ever. Come, and inflame my heart with Thy Divine Love. Let the fire of Thy Love consume within me whatever is displeasing to Thee. Let all my thoughts, words, and actions be steeped in Thy love, so that, henceforth, I may do nothing but what is pleasing to Thee, O sweet Spirit of Love and Holiness.

Invocation of the B. V. Mary and the Saints. Holy Mary, Mother of God, Immaculate Spouse of the Holy Ghost, given to me by Jesus to be my mother also, assist me now by thy powerful intercession that I may worthily receive the most Holy and most Adorable Spirit of God.

Glorious St. Michael and all ye heavenly Spirits, St. Joseph, all ye holy Apostles and Disciples of our Lord, my good Guardian Angel and holy Patrons, all ye Saints of God: assist me now by your united prayers before the Throne of God that I may worthily receive the Holy Ghost in this most holy Sacrament.

Holy Mary, all ye holy Apostles, Disciples and faithful followers of our Lord who were favored to receive the Holy Ghost on the day of Pentecost in such a singular manner, pray for me, that, as far as possible, I may be animated with the same feelings of love, wonder, and desire with which you were animated so that the Holy Ghost may produce within me the same wonderful results according to my particular needs and condition of life.

Aspiration. Lord, God the Holy Ghost, I am not worthy that Thou shouldst deign to come to me. But what am I without Thee? And what can I do without Thee? Come then, and fill the heart of Thy unworthy servant and enkindle within me the fire of Thy love. Amen.

3. A Prayer for the Seven Gifts of the Holy Ghost

O Divine Spirit, in harmony with the Prayer of Prayers, taught us by Jesus, our Divine Master, I humbly beseech Thee:

(1) Deign to bestow upon me the gift of Wisdom, that I may hallow Thy Name, and cause others to respect it. Amen.

Glory be.

(2) Deign to bestow upon me the gift of Understanding, that I may fathom the secrets of Thy Kingdom and help to spread it among men. Amen.

Glory be.

(3) Deign to bestow upon me the gift of Counsel, that I may be able to do Thy Will on earth as it is done in heaven. Amen.

Glory be.

(4) Deign to bestow upon me the gift of Knowledge, that I may learn how to esteem, and worthily receive, my daily substantial Bread, Jesus Himself, in the Blessed Sacrament of the Altar. Amen.

Glory be.

(5) Deign to bestow upon me the gift of Piety, that I may forgive others so as to obtain from Thee forgiveness for myself. Amen.

Glory be.

(6) Deign to bestow upon me the gift of Fortitude, that I may not fall into temptation, and may overcome all the enemies of my soul. Amen.

Glory be.

(7) Deign to bestow upon me the gift of Fear, that I may always and everywhere shun all deliberate dangerous occasions of sin and be delivered from evil. Amen.

Glory be.

4. Rite of Confirmation

The Bishop wearing over his rochet an amice, stole, and cope of white, and having a mitre on his head, proceeds to the faldstool, before the middle of the Altar, or has it placed for him in some other convenient place, and sits thereon with his back to the Altar and his face towards the people, holding his crosier in his left hand. He washes his hands, still sitting; then laying aside his mitre, he arises, and standing with his face towards the persons to be confirmed, and having his hands joined before his breast (the persons to be confirmed kneeling, and having their hands also joined before their breasts), he says:

May the Holy Ghost descend upon you, and may the power of the Most High preserve you from sins.

R. Amen.

Then signing himself with the sign of the Cross, from his forehead to his breast, he says:

V. Our help is in the name of the Lord.
R. Who hath made heaven and earth.
V. O Lord, hear my prayer.
R. And let my cry come unto Thee.
V. The Lord be with you.
R. And with thy spirit.

Then, with hands extended towards those to be confirmed, he says:

Let us pray:

Almighty and eternal God, Who hast vouchsafed to regenerate these Thy servants by water and the Holy Ghost, and hast given unto them forgiveness of all their sins; send forth from heaven upon them Thy sevenfold Spirit, the Holy Comforter.

R. Amen.

V. The Spirit of Wisdom and Understanding.

R. Amen.

V. The Spirit of Counsel and Fortitude.

R. Amen.

V. The Spirit of Knowledge and Piety.

R. Amen.

Fill them with the spirit of Thy Fear, and sign them with the sign of the Cross of Christ, in Thy mercy, unto life eternal. Through the same our Lord Jesus Christ, Thy Son, who liveth and reigneth with Thee in the unity of the same Holy Ghost, God, world without end.

R. Amen.

The Bishop, sitting on the faldstool, or, if the number of persons to be confirmed requires it, standing, with his mitre on his head, confirms them, arranged in rows and kneeling in order. He inquires separately the name of each person to be confirmed, who is presented to him by the godfather or godmother, kneeling; and having dipped the end of the thumb of his right hand in chrism, he says:

I sign thee with the sign of the Cross.

Whilst saying these words, he makes the sign of the Cross, with his thumb, on the forehead of the person to be confirmed, and then says:

And I confirm thee with the chrism of salvation. In the name of the Father, and of the Son, and of the Holy Ghost.

R. Amen.

Then he strikes the person confirmed gently on the cheek, saying:

Peace be with thee.

When all have been confirmed, the bishop wipes his hands with bread-crumbs, and washes them over a basin. In the meantime the following antiphon is said or sung by the clergy:

Confirm, O God, that which Thou hast wrought in us, from Thy holy temple which is in Jerusalem.

R. Glory be to the Father, etc.

Then the antiphon Confirm, O God is repeated; after which the Bishop, laying aside his mitre, rises up, and standing towards the Altar, with his hands joined before his breast, says:

O Lord, show Thy mercy upon us.

R. And grant us Thy salvation.

V. O Lord, hear my prayer.

R. And let my cry come unto Thee.

V. The Lord be with you.

R. And with thy spirit.

Then, with his hands still joined before his breast, and all the persons confirmed devoutly kneeling, he says:

Let us pray:

O God, who didst give Thine Apostles the Holy Ghost, and didst ordain that by them and their successors He should be given to the rest of the faithful; look mercifully upon our unworthy service; and grant that the hearts of those whose foreheads we have anointed with holy chrism, and signed with the sign of the Holy Cross, may, by the same Holy Spirit coming down upon them, and graciously abiding within them, be made the temple of His glory. Who with the Father and the same Holy Ghost, livest and reignest, God, world without end.

R. Amen.

Then he says:

Behold, thus shall every man be blessed that feareth the Lord.

And, turning to the persons confirmed, he makes over them the sign of the Cross, saying:

May the Lord bless you out of Zion, that you may see the good things of Jerusalem all the days of your life, and may have life everlasting.

R. Amen.

5. Thanksgiving after Confirmation

Acts of Adoration, Love and Thanksgiving. O Divine Spirit, Thou hast been pleased to visit me, Thy unworthy servant, and to take up Thy abode within my soul and my very body. Thou hast dedicated my soul and my body as Thy living temple. Thou hast consecrated me wholly and entirely to God's holy service. Thou hast lavished upon me Thy heavenly gifts to make me a perfect Christian and a valiant soldier of Jesus Christ.

Yet Who art Thou, my Lord and my God? And who am I? Thou art a God of infinite Perfections, of infinite Holiness, and Purity. And I am nothing but dust and ashes. I have nothing of my own but sin and misery.

I humbly bow down and adore Thee present within the sanctuary of my poor soul. Upon Thee I depend for everything. Upon Thee I lean for everything. May I be wholly Thine for evermore.

O how can I ever thank Thee sufficiently for all Thou hast done for me already; and, in a special manner, for what Thou hast done for me on this very day. Thou hast poured forth Thyself upon my whole being. Thou hast given Thyself to me to be a pledge of my eternal inheritance. Thou hast Thyself become unto me a seal unto the day of redemption. Thou hast replenished me with Thy sevenfold grace so that I may be able to practice every virtue and become fruitful in every good work. Deign to accept my most sincere and humble thanks I now offer to Thee from the very depth of my soul.

I call upon the Blessed Virgin Mary, Thy Immaculate Spouse, upon all the Angels and Saints, upon all Thy faithful servants and upon all creatures to thank, love, adore, and praise Thee in union with me.

I offer up to Thee the fervent acts of love, praise, adoration and thanksgiving which were offered to Thee by Mary, in union with the Apostles and other followers of our Lord on the day of Pentecost.

I offer to Thee the infinite homage of love Thou eternally receivest from the Father and the Son.

Deign to accept the oblation of my whole being, which I now offer up to Thee in the sweet name of Jesus and through the pure hands of Mary,

May I ever abide in Thy Love! May I never grieve or offend Thee! May I manifest my love for Thee by an ever increasing readiness to do Thy most Holy Will!

An act of Petition. O Divine Spirit of grace and prayer, Thou art the Fount of all Goodness, the Source of all tender mercies. Behold and pity the poverty and wretchedness of Thy lowly servant.

Thou art the Father of the poor. Enrich my poverty out of the infinite treasures of Thy Love and Mercy.

Thou art the Giver of all gifts. Bestow upon me whatever Thou knowest to be needful to me for soul and body.

Thou art the Light of hearts. Enkindle within me the fire of Thy Divine Love which is the light of my heart. Thou art of all Comforters the best. Fill me with heavenly comfort whenever I am sad and weary.

Thou art now my soul's sweet Guest. Oh! never again depart from me, but stay with me always. Be Thou my soul's refreshment in time and in eternity.

In toil and labor, be Thou my Repose. In strife and conflict, be Thou my shelter. In sorrow and sadness, be Thou my solace.

Be Thou the Light of my soul, that, through Thee, I may come to know God on earth, and see Him face to face in heaven.

Without Thee, I am nothing but sin and misery.

Do Thou, therefore, cleanse me from sin, heal the wounds inflicted in my soul by sin, and grant me Thy grace to do Thy Holy Will. Bend my stubborn will to yield to Thine. Fill my cold heart with Thy burning Love. Be Thou my guide and safeguard on the road to heaven.

Bestow upon me the fullness of Thy seven gifts of Wisdom, Understanding, Counsel, Fortitude, Knowledge, Piety, and the Fear of the Lord, so that I may practice more diligently Faith, Hope, and Charity, and every other virtue, and produce within the garden of my soul Thy twelve most holy fruits; especially joy, peace, patience, and modesty.

Above all, give me the grace to persevere in Thy Divine Service unto the end and die a good and happy death, so that, in heaven, I may forever be happy with Thee together with the Father and the Son, to Whom be honor and glory for ever and ever, Amen.

Do not forget to pray to the Divine Spirit to grant you that particular grace you need most . . . to strengthen you against that particular temptation which assails you most frequently . . . to keep you from that particular sin to which you are most liable . . . so that you may indeed be a perfect Christian and a valiant soldier of Jesus Christ.

Pray also for all the faithful that they may increase in faith and virtue.

Pray for the spread of the Christian Faith. Pray for the welfare of the Catholic Church. Pray for the chief Pastor, the Pope, and all Bishops and Priests.

Ask the Blessed Virgin Mary and all the Angels and Saints to join their prayers with yours.

Endeavor to bear in mind the solemn obligations contracted in Confirmation and endeavor to keep them by the grace of the Holy Ghost.

Remember the anniversary day of your Confirmation and keep it with all fervor and devotion.

Cultivate special devotion to the Holy Ghost, and endeavor to spread the same among others.

6. Prayer on the Anniversary of Confirmation

(May also be used frequently during the year.)

Thanks be unto Thee, O my God, for all Thy infinite goodness, and especially for that love that Thou hast shown unto me on the day of my Confirmation.

I give Thee thanks that Thou didst send down Thy Holy Spirit into my soul with all His gifts and graces. O may He take full possession of me for ever; may His divine unction cause my face to shine; may His heavenly wisdom reign in my heart, His understanding enlighten my darkness, His counsel guide me, His fortitude strengthen me, His knowledge instruct me, His piety make me fervent, His Divine fear keep me from all evil.

Drive from my soul, O Lord, all that would defile it. Give me grace to be Thy faithful soldier, that having fought the good fight of faith, I may be brought to the crown of everlasting life, through the merits of Thy dearly beloved Son, our Savior, Jesus Christ. Amen.

XV. Devout Exercise of Reparation for the Sins Committed Against the Holy Ghost

1. Notice

"Grieve not the Spirit of God."
"Extinguish not the Spirit."

Each sin, however slight, grieves the Divine Spirit; for sin is in direct opposition to God's Holy will. Mortal sin, however, not merely grieves Him, but also extinguishes Him, inasmuch as it expels Him from the soul of man wherein He dwells by His Divine grace. Yet there are certain sins which are, in a special manner, opposed to the Holy Ghost. These are: Presuming on God's mercy; Despair; Resisting the known truth; Envying another's spiritual good; Obstinacy in sin; and Final Impenitence. If you are devout to the Holy Ghost, you will endeavor to make some reparation to the Divine Spirit for these particular sins. In so doing, you will perform an act both pleasing to God and beneficial to yourself.

2. Preparatory Prayer

✛ In the name of the Father, and of the Son, and of the Holy Ghost. Amen.

An Act of Sorrow:—O God, the Holy Ghost, Divine Spirit of Mercy, Truth, and Holiness! It pains me to think that there are men who directly oppose Thee. Yet,

I, too, have, at times, offended Thee by my sins. I now implore Thy mercy and forgiveness; and I promise, with the help of Thy Holy grace, never to offend Thee again.

The Invocation:—Come, O Holy Ghost, fill the hearts of Thy faithful; and kindle in them the fire of Thy love.

V. Send forth Thy Spirit, and they shall be created.

R. And Thou shalt renew the face of the earth.

Let us pray:

O God, Who, by the light of Thy Holy Spirit, didst teach the hearts of Thy faithful: grant us, by the same Spirit, to have a right judgment in all things, and evermore to rejoice in His holy comfort. Through Christ our Lord. Amen.

3. First Reflection—The sin of Presuming on God's Mercy

Let us consider the insult offered to God, the Holy Ghost, by those who offend Him through the sin of presumption.

Left to ourselves, we can absolutely do nothing towards obtaining eternal salvation. Now, it is the special office of the Holy Ghost to apply to our souls the means of salvation prepared by our Divine Redeemer. Yet we, also, on our part must do something. We must be diligent in employing these means and be faithful in cooperating with Divine grace. The presumptuous, however, vainly imagine they will obtain eternal salvation without making use of the means placed at their disposal by the Holy Ghost. Hence arises their neglect of prayer, of hearing the word of God, of assisting at Holy Mass, and of receiving the Sacraments. They expect to avoid sin, without carefully shunning the dangerous occasions of sin. Having fallen into grievous sin, they willfully remain in that unhappy condition, heaping sin upon sin; and, all the time, they rely upon a death-bed repentance, fondly consoling themselves with the idea that God is too good to allow them to be lost for ever, and suffer endless misery. Thus they deliberately blind themselves, and offend the Holy Ghost in a special manner, by positively casting aside the means of salvation so bountifully held out to them by the same Divine Spirit. They certainly outrage His Divine goodness and liberality in an eminent degree, and place themselves, as far as they are concerned, in a most lamentable condition, since nothing short of a miracle can save them. May they be roused from that unhappy state before it is too late! And may we be ever distrustful of ourselves, fervently imploring the aid of the Holy Ghost on all occasions and faithfully corresponding with His Divine grace.

4. Prayer of Reparation

V. We long to adore, praise, bless, and glorify Thee, O Most Adorable Spirit of the Father, and of the Son, God the Holy Ghost.

R. And we desire to repair, by our fervor and zeal in Thy Divine service, the insults and injuries offered Thy Divine Majesty.

V. Create in me a clean heart, O God: and renew a right spirit within me.

R. Cast me not away from Thy face; and take not Thy Holy Spirit from me.

Let us pray:

O God the Holy Ghost, Who art but little known and loved by men, grant, we beseech Thee, that, through the merits of Jesus, our Divine Redeemer, and through the intercession of Mary, Thy Immaculate Spouse, we may come to know more and more Thy Divine Personality, and to realize more fully Thine adorable Presence, Power, and Love: so that we may, with our whole minds and hearts, and the energy of our entire being, for ever glorify Thee, together with the Father, and the Son, one God, in perfect Trinity, world without end. Amen.

Our Father. Hail Mary. Glory.

N.B.—Before each consideration say the preparatory prayer and conclude with the prayer of reparation.

5. Second Reflection—The sin of Despair

Let us consider the insult offered to God the Holy Ghost by those who offend Him through the sin of despair

God loves all men. "With an everlasting love have I loved thee," He assures each one. God the Father so loved all men as to give up for their salvation His only-begotten Son. God the Son so loved all men as to become man for their sake and shed each single drop of His most Precious Blood on the Cross of Calvary. The Holy Ghost so loves all men as to condescend to abide within their hearts and souls, and to sanctify them by His Divine Presence. Who, then, can despair of obtaining mercy and pardon for his sins, let them be ever so great? "As I live, saith the Lord, I desire not the death of the wicked, but that the wicked turn from his ways and live." . . . "If your sins be as scarlet, they shall be made whiter than snow." Who can despair when he reflects upon God's intense yearning for souls, as He fondly exclaims again and again: "Turn ye, turn ye from your evil ways, and why will ye die?" For "the Son of Man came to seek that which was lost." No sin is too great, for "with the Lord there is plentiful redemption." . . . "Go, show yourselves to the priests." . . . "He that shall confess his sins, and forsake them, shall obtain mercy." Have courage, then, poor sinful soul! "I am with you." . . . "My grace is sufficient for you." How great, therefore, is the sin of those who deliberately distrust God to such an extent as to despair entirely of eternal salvation! By this sin, God the Holy Ghost is offended in a special manner, since it is His particular office to apply to the souls of poor sinners the infinite merits of Christ, to rescue them from the slavery of sin, and preserve them from eternal woe. The Holy Ghost is the Power of God. They who despair willfully reject the aid of His Almighty Power, The Holy Ghost is goodness, love, and mercy itself. They who despair deny and outrage these Divine attributes. What an insult to the Divine Spirit! What a dreadful state for those who thus despair? Who or what can save them? May they turn to God in all confidence and repentance before despair has fully taken hold of them. As for ourselves, we will put all our trust in God's infinite mercy and goodness. If we truly hope in Him, we shall never be confounded. Yet, at the same time, we must not forget to place our hope on a solid foundation by faithfully performing whatever God enables us to do by the assistance of His Divine grace.

6. Third Reflection—The sin of Resisting the Known Truth

Let us consider the insult offered to God the Holy Ghost by those who offend Him through the sin of resisting the known truth.

The Holy Ghost is called by our Divine Lord the Spirit of Truth. "I will send Him to you, the Spirit of Truth. . . . He will teach you all things." There are men, however, who not only endeavor to avoid hearing the truth, but who deliberately refuse to accept it when it is announced to them by Divine authority, or again willfully reject it after having once embraced it. There are men who, in their own mind, are fully persuaded that the Catholic Church is the true Church of Jesus Christ, and yet fail to join the one true Fold. There are men who boast of being Catholics and say they believe in God's word, but who gainsay it in practice by their evil lives, thereby bringing discredit on the Catholic Faith and keeping many an earnest, well-meaning soul that is searching for the truth away from the true Church. All such, together with those who directly attack, calumniate and misrepresent the known truth, grossly insult and outrage the Spirit of Truth. For it is through the Holy Ghost that, at any time, Divine Revelation has been made to mankind. It was the Holy Ghost, who, of old, spoke to men through the Patriarchs and Prophets. It was the Holy Ghost who inspired and guided the sacred writers of Holy Scripture and thus gave us the written word of God. Nay, Jesus Christ Himself, the Eternal Word, the Eternal Truth, has been given to us by the power and operation of the Holy Ghost. The Church of Christ, which is the ground and pillar of truth, has been brought into existence, is animated and directed by the Holy Ghost. And the Sovereign Pontiff, the Vicar of Christ, and visible Head of His Church, is the infallible mouth-piece of the Holy Ghost. Whosoever, therefore, resists the known truth sins directly against the Holy Ghost. He hears the voice of God, but deliberately hardens his heart, and, in his willful blindness, prefers the devil, the father of lies, to the Holy Ghost, the Spirit of Truth. Would that all men heard and followed the voice of the Spirit of Truth! "Today, if you shall hear His voice, harden not your hearts . . . but listen attentively to His awful word." But who is the living, outward voice of the Holy Ghost? The Catholic Church, and, in a special manner, the Sovereign Pontiff. May all men be sensible to the manifest claims of the Catholic Church, the pillar and ground of truth; and may all recognize in the Sovereign Pontiff the infallible mouth-piece of the Holy Ghost. As for ourselves, let our Catholic Faith ever remain steadfast and unshaken, since it is the infallible utterance of the Holy Ghost, the Spirit of Truth.

7. Fourth Reflection—The sin of Envying another's spiritual good

Let us consider the insult offered to God the Holy Ghost by those who offend Him through the sin of envying their neighbor's spiritual good.

Who can understand the infinite Bounty of the Holy Ghost, the substantial Love of the Father and of the Son! He never wearies in bestowing blessings on all men. Whatever favor is received by them is an outpouring of His boundless love. Yet the Holy Ghost is absolutely free to give to whomsoever He wishes, and in whatever measure He pleases. To all, He gives an abundance of Divine grace, sufficient to enable each one to save his immortal soul. But with regard to some, He is more liberal than with regard to others. Some are literally overwhelmed with His choicest gifts and privileges. But has He not a perfect right to do so? "The Spirit breatheth where He will" . . . "dividing to everyone according as He will." And who dare criticise His dealings with men, or censure His judgments in the distribution of His Divine gifts! Is not this a blasphemy against the Holy Ghost! Yet this is the sin committed by those who are envious of their neighbor's spiritual good. They murmur on account of seeing themselves less favored by God than others. They accuse God of partiality, and even injustice, as though they had been robbed or deprived, as due to them, of whatever good they see in their neighbor; or else they attempt to lower or destroy the virtues and good qualities of their fellowmen by attributing them to hypocrisy, or some other unworthy motive, as did the Jews when they ascribed the miracles wrought by Jesus to the power of

Beelzebub, the prince of devils. Envy is one of the special sins of the devil. Hence, they who are envious of their neighbor's spiritual good, follow the evil spirit in a particular manner, and thus directly oppose the Holy Ghost, the Spirit of Love and Charity. "By the envy of the devil, death came into the world: and they follow him that are of his side." May God, in His mercy, open the eyes of the envious that they may clearly see on whose side they are, and will be for ever, unless they repent of their sin! As for ourselves, may God, in His infinite goodness, ever keep us in His Love, and preserve us from the spirit of envy.

8. Fifth Reflection—The sin of Obstinacy of sin

Let us consider the insult offered to God the Holy Ghost by those who offend Him through obstinacy in sin.

What is there God has not done for the eternal welfare of our immortal souls? He, the God of all goodness, made us to His own image and likeness, and destined us to become the sons of His adoption. He has now placed us on this earth to know, love, and serve Him with all filial reverence and submission, so that, after this short term of probation here below, we may enter upon our eternal inheritance in heaven above. For our sake did Jesus Christ, Who was conceived of the Holy Ghost and born of the Blessed Virgin Mary, come on

this earth to suffer and to die. For by sin we had for-
feited our right to heaven and been doomed to death
and all misery. At the price of His Most Precious Blood,
Jesus Christ ransomed us from that dreadful slavery of
sin and Satan, and merited for us, once more, all the
graces necessary for our eternal salvation. For our sake
has the Holy Ghost been given unto us to abide in
our souls, to beget them to a new life, and seal them
unto the day of redemption. He it is that fits out our
souls with grace and holiness, endows them with His
Divine gifts, and patiently awaits the fruit of His labor,
which is to manifest itself by a life of good works on
earth and obtain for us an everlasting reward in heaven.
Now, they who deliberately return to the commission
of sin, and who obstinately remain in sin, by that very
fact cast away the graces and blessings of God the Holy
Ghost, and thus outrage Him in a singular manner.
The Divine Spirit of Love calls upon them—invites
them—pleads with them—threatens them. But all to
no purpose. They willfully prefer sin to virtue, darkness
to light. They would rather wallow in the mire of sin
than walk in the path of virtue. They prefer their souls
to be an abode of the demons of iniquity than of the
Spirit of Holiness. They want to lead a life of sin, and
will not employ the means of reconciliation. Hence,
they positively despise the Divine invitations, laugh at
the Divine warnings, and reject every offer of pardon

and mercy. What an outrage to the Divine Spirit! What base ingratitude! Not to speak of the fearful danger to which the obstinate in sin expose their own immortal souls! How can they be saved as long as they remain in that awful state? No wonder that, as a rule, God gives them up entirely "to a reprobate sense," and "the desires of their heart," and lets them "die in their sin." As for ourselves, we will loathe and detest all sin, and flee from it as from a poisonous serpent. Yet should we ever have the misfortune to fall, let us beware remaining in sin and putting off our conversion from day to day. God is good; yet He is also just. Let us heed the warning of the Holy Ghost: "Delay not to be converted to the Lord . . . and add not sin upon sin. . . . For His wrath shall come on a sudden, and, in the time of His vengeance, He will destroy."

9. Sixth Reflection—The sin of Final Impenitence

Let us consider the insult offered to God the Holy Ghost by those who offend Him through the sin of final impenitence.

Final impenitence is, as a rule, the natural outcome and the just punishment of obstinacy in sin. For by remaining obstinate to the very last, such as these positively refuse every tender call to repentance; they spurn the ministry of the priest; they reject the powerful and consoling aids of the Sacraments; they remain deaf to every entreaty of their friends; they simply will not turn to God and implore His forgiveness for a life of sin and iniquity. This they will do while stretched out on their death-bed, knowing full well that their days are numbered, and that their last hour is close at hand. Thus they defy God with death staring at them to the face, nay, with hell open at their feet, ready to swallow them up. They know it; their eyes are wide open; nay, while still breathing in the body, they seem to have already crossed the threshold of eternity. They will tell you themselves that their doom has already been sealed. And hence they will cry out in their fits of despair that all is useless, that nothing can save them, that they will be lost, that they are lost already. Such is the usual end of those wretched souls. There is no need for God to condemn them; they signed their own death-warrant long ago, and they deliberately cast themselves headlong into everlasting perdition. Alas! all that God, in His Love, ever did for their eternal salvation, has, by that sin, been made void and useless. Alas! the toils and labors of a God made man, the shedding of His Most Precious Blood, that agonizing death of His on the cross, have, by that sin, been rendered fruitless and superfluous. Alas! the infinite Love of the Holy Ghost has, by that sin, been spurned and rejected for ever. Hence God cries aloud: "Hear, O ye heavens, and give ear, O earth. I have brought up children, and exalted them. But they have despised Me." Final impenitence is, indeed, the climax of all the sins opposed to the Holy Ghost. How great is its enormity! How frightful its consequences! No human tongue can ever tell. We can only gather an idea from the awful spectacle exhibited by one dying in final impenitence. May God, in His infinite mercy, grant us the grace so to live as to ensure a good and a happy death.

XVI. Novena in Honor of God the Holy Ghost

1. The first Novena

The first Novena we have knowledge of is the one recorded in the first Chapter of the Acts of the Apostles.

That Novena was made in preparation for the coming of the Holy Ghost, on the day of Pentecost. It was, therefore, *a Novena in honor of God the Holy Ghost.*

The persons making this Novena were the Blessed Virgin Mary, the Apostles and Disciples of our Lord, the Holy Women and the other faithful believers, in all about a hundred and twenty souls. They represented at that time *the entire Church* of Jesus Christ. They formed the material of the Church's edifice which was to be completed and quickened into life by the coming of the Holy Ghost.

The Novena was made *at the express command of Jesus*

Christ, Who had told them not to depart from Jerusalem until they had received the promised Paraclete.

The manner in which they made this Novena was by *prayer and retirement*. It was, in fact, a spiritual retreat.

The effects of that Novena were simply marvelous. Personally, they were all filled with the Holy Ghost. They received, moreover, not only the full outpouring of His Divine grace, but also very extraordinary gifts and favors. The Apostles and Disciples, in particular, were endowed with fortitude and eloquence to preach the Gospel of their Divine Master throughout the whole world. On that day the Church was brought forth into existence through the coming of the Holy Spirit, the Life-giver, Who abides within her, that she may effectually carry on the work of men's salvation to the end of time.

What *conclusions* may you draw from this?

If the Church prepared for the first coming of the Holy Ghost by a solemn and public Novena at the command of Jesus, her Divine Founder, what is more befitting than that the Church at the present day should commemorate the anniversary of that eventful day by making a solemn and public Novena in preparation for the day of Pentecost! Was it not, therefore, just and reasonable that the Sovereign Pontiff, the Head of the Church and Vicar of Jesus Christ, should ordain such a public and solemn Novena to be celebrated in every public church throughout the entire Catholic world wherever it was possible and convenient to do so!

And if you yourself should at any time stand in need of some special grace of the Holy Ghost, what more efficacious means can you employ than making a Novena in honor of God the Holy Ghost!

2. How to make the Novena

Bear in mind that the end of the Novena is to draw down upon yourself some special grace of the Holy Ghost, or rather to draw down the Holy Ghost Himself; for the Holy Ghost comes to you afresh each time He bestows His Divine grace upon you. But in order to draw down the Holy Ghost you must do something to attract Him. And how will you attract Him? By prayer and retirement, after the example of the Blessed Virgin Mary, of the Apostles and other followers of our Lord.

First, then, you must prepare your soul for the coming of the Holy Spirit *by prayer*: that is, by asking Him directly in fervent and earnest words to come and visit your poor soul and grant it that particular favor or blessing you desire, whether for yourself or others.

But your prayers must be animated chiefly by *an ardent longing* to receive the Holy Ghost. You must excite within your heart a burning desire to be filled with the Holy Spirit of God. Reflect upon His ineffable Goodness, His boundless Love, His entrancing Beauty, His store of Truth, His treasures of Grace. Think on what He has done for you already and what He is still anxious to do for you. Remember His Divine Presence within you, and consider that which it implies. Each day of the Novena you should, therefore, read something concerning the Holy Ghost and make a little meditation upon what you have read.

Yet take care to remove also every hindrance to the coming of the Holy Ghost. Your prayers and meditations should, therefore, be accompanied with lively sentiments of true sorrow for all your past sins, failings and shortcomings. Not only should you be free from actual sin, but also from all attachment to sin. To this end let your acts of sorrow and contrition not be confined merely to the time of your humble confession, but let them be lasting and abiding and of such a nature as to root up all attachment to sin and correct your faults and sinful habits.

The other condition for preparing your soul for the Holy Ghost is *retirement*. If your position and station in life will allow you to retire altogether for a little while, and make a spiritual retreat, so much the better. But if you cannot actually retire from your ordinary occupations, at least cultivate, as far as possible, interior recollection, and endeavor to acquire and preserve interior peace of mind. Whenever anything disturbs you, it arises either from an undue attachment to something you possess, or from an undue desire and craving after something you do not possess. Moderate your affections and desires, keep them within due limits, according to God's holy will, and you will enjoy a peaceful calm, which nothing can disturb. And when your heart is thus at rest, the Divine Spirit will come and abide therein and fill it with every blessing.

3. Particular directions

If the Novena is made publicly by all the members of a parish, the Reverend Pastor himself will be the best judge as to how to conduct the Novena according to the condition and needs of his parishioners.

Let him speak to his people beforehand of the meaning, importance and advantages of the Novena.

Let special prayers in honor of God the Holy Ghost be offered up publicly each day, and let something be read, or a short discourse be given, concerning the Divine Spirit.

Let the people be advised how to conduct themselves during the Novena after the example of the Bl. Virgin Mary, the Apostles, and other followers of our Lord, so as to draw down upon themselves an abundance of Divine blessings. Let them not forget to approach the Sacraments of Confession and Communion.

If you cannot assist at the public Novena, do what you can in private. Try and follow the directions as closely as possible by yourself.

To make your Novena more efficacious, join with others, either actually, or at least in spirit. How beautiful a sight it would be to see all the members of the same family join together in making a Novena in honor of God the Holy Ghost. Certainly that house would be blessed most singularly.

Remember also that a number of indulgences are granted for making this Novena, whether in public or in private, whether in preparation for the day of Pentecost, or at any other time during the year.

4. Pope Leo XIII on the Novena of Pentecost

"We decree and command that throughout the whole Catholic Church, this year, and in every subsequent year, a Novena shall be made before Whit Sunday, in all parish churches, and also, if the local ordinaries think fit, in other churches end oratories.

"To all who take part in this Novena and duly pray for our intention, We grant for each day an indulgence of seven years and seven quarantines; moreover, a plenary indulgence on any of the days of the Novena, or on Whit Sunday itself, or on any day during the Octave, provided they shall have received the Sacraments of Penance and the Holy Eucharist, and devoutly prayed for our intention.

"We will that those who are legitimately prevented from attending the Novena, or who are in places where the devotions cannot, in the judgment of the ordinary, be conveniently carried out in Church, shall equally enjoy the same benefits, provided they make the Novena privately and observe the other conditions.

"Moreover, We are pleased to grant, in perpetuity, from the Treasury of the Church, that whosoever, daily during the Octave of Pentecost up to Trinity Sunday inclusive, offer again publicly or privately any prayers, according to their devotion, to the Holy Ghost, and satisfy the above conditions, shall a second time gain each of the same indulgences.

"All these indulgences We also permit to be applied to the suffrage of the souls in Purgatory."

Encyclical, May 9th, 1897.

5. Reflection for each day of the Novena

There are a number of ecclesiastical hymns in honor of the Holy Ghost. The sequence *Veni, Sancte Spiritus* said during the mass on Pentecost Sunday holds undoubtedly the first place. How simple, and yet, how beautiful are its thoughts and expressions! How touching and sweet its petitions and aspirations! It is the cry of the poor wayfaring soul from the depth of its miseries and afflictions to Him Who alone can bestow peace and comfort in time and eternity.

A literal translation of the sequence is herewith given, as no metrical version can ever give the full meaning of the original. It may be used as a daily prayer during the Novena. The explanation which follows gives sufficient matter for a brief meditation for each day of the Novena.

6. The Sequence *Veni, Sancte Spiritus*

(Literal version.)

Come, O Holy Spirit,
    And from heaven send forth
        Of Thy Light one ray.

Come, Thou Father of the poor,
    Come, Thou Giver of gifts,
        Come, Thou Light of hearts.

O Thou, best Comforter,
    Thou, the soul's sweet Guest,
        Sweet Refreshment Thou.

Thou art Rest in labor,
    Thou art Shelter from the heat,
        Thou art Solace in our weeping.

O Thou, most blissful Light,
    Fill the inmost hearts
        Of Thy faithful.

Unless Thou givest,
    There is naught in man,
        Naught but what is sinful.

Wash Thou what is stained,
    Water what is parched,
        Heal Thou what is wounded.

Bend Thou what is rigid;
    Warm Thou what is cold;
        Guide Thou what is erring.

Give unto Thy faithful,
    Who put their trust in Thee,
        Thy most sacred sevenfold gift.

Grant Thou virtue its reward;
    Grant a happy end;
        Grant eternal happiness.
                Amen. Alleluia.

7. First Day of the Novena

1. *"Come, O Holy Spirit."* The term "Holy Spirit" expresses both the Personality of the Third Person of the Blessed Trinity as well as His Divine Mission.

His Divine Personality. The First Person of the Blessed

Trinity is called the Father, and the Second the Son, on account of the mutual relationship between them, the Son being begotten of the Father from all eternity. The Third Divine Person, however, is simply called the Holy Ghost, the Holy Spirit. This does not, at first sight, appear to be a distinctive name, and yet it is so. As the Second Person proceeds from the First by way of generation, and is, for that reason called the Son of the Eternal Father, so the Third Divine Person proceeds from the First and from the Second by way of spiration, or breathing, and is, therefore, rightly called the Breath, or Spirit, of the Father and of the Son. Again, as the Son is the expression of the Eternal Mind of the Father, and is, for that reason, called the Eternal Word, the Eternal Wisdom, the Eternal Truth, so the Third Person is the expression of the Divine Will of the Father and of the Son, and is, therefore, called the Uncreated Love and Holiness of the Godhead. Hence the term "Holy Spirit," or the Divine Spirit of Love and Holiness, fully expresses His Divine Personality.

His Divine Mission. As the Son proceeds from the Father, and has, by Him, been sent on earth to redeem mankind and merit for men Divine grace, so the Holy Ghost, who proceeds from the Father and the Son, has been sent on earth by the Father and the Son to sanctify men, by applying to their souls the merits of their Divine Redeemer. By His personal indwelling in the hearts of men, He clothes their souls with the garment of sanctifying grace, and, by His constant assistance, He gives them all the actual graces they need to work out their eternal salvation. He is, therefore, rightly called the Holy Spirit; for He is the Spirit, the Breath of God, quickening the souls of men into a new life, the life of justice and holiness. Hence Holy Scripture, speaking of the creation of man, says: "God breathed into his face the breath of life, and man became a living soul;" and concerning the foundation of the Church, or the regeneration of man, it says: "And there came a sound from heaven, as of a mighty wind coming. . . and they were all filled with the Holy Ghost," God the Father and the Son, so to speak, breathing down the Divine Spirit to take up His abode in the hearts of men and filling them with His Divine Love and Holiness.

Then go on your knees, and adore the Holy Ghost with all your heart and soul; for He is your God, consubstantial, co-eternal with the Father and the Son, to Whom be honor and glory for ever more.

Thank Him for all He is doing for you; for He is your Sanctifier. To Him you owe everything directly. Be guided by Him. Yield to His Divine operations. Make use of the graces and blessings He bestows upon you.

2. If the Holy Ghost be sent, why ask Him to come? If He has already taken possession of your soul by His

od gave you freedom, and He so respects this gift that
He does nothing in your regard against your own free
will. True, He gave you existence, and, along with your
existence, countless blessings of soul and body, without
first consulting you. But ever since the moment that
you were able to employ the gift of freedom, "He has
left you in the hand of your own counsel," so that now
He will not save you unless you, of your own free will,
desire it. Therefore, although the Holy Ghost has been
sent to you, He will not come to abide with you, unless
you are willing to receive Him and say to Him with
all humility: Come, Holy Ghost! fill my soul with Thy
Divine Presence. If you desire an increase of sanctifying
grace, again you must say: Come, Holy Ghost! do
Thou strengthen, within me, the life of grace. If you
need the assistance of His actual grace, again you must
say: Come, Holy Ghost! help me by the all-powerful
aid of Thy Divine grace. If ever you have the misfortune to drive Him away from your soul by grievous sin,
then more than ever must you cry out to Him: Come,
Holy Ghost! fill my heart with sorrow and repentance,
and restore unto me the life of grace and the joy of
Thy salvation.

Hence be ever constant in imploring the aid of the
Holy Ghost. Make it a practice to call upon the Divine

Spirit at once whenever you need His special assistance: Come, Holy Ghost! assist me by Thy holy grace. Incline unto mine aid, O God. O Lord, make haste to help me.

3. *"And from heaven send forth of Thy light one ray."* When the Holy Ghost bestows upon you His grace, He first illumines your mind to show you what to do or to avoid, and then moves and strengthens your will, so that, of your own free will, you may do what you know to be right. The Holy Ghost may, under this aspect, be said to be to your soul what the sun is to this physical world. The sun primarily gives light, but along with the light, it also imparts warmth and heat, renders the earth fertile to yield fruit in due season, and fills all terrestrial beings with joy and gladness. Thus, in like manner, when you are under the genial influence of God the Holy Ghost, your mind is enlightened, your heart is set on fire with Divine charity, your soul is enabled to bring forth fruits of virtue and good works, and your entire being is, in consequence, flooded with peace and joy in the Lord.

But again bear in mind, that grace is not given to you unless you ask for it. Hence once more you are taught to look up to the Holy Ghost on His throne of Love above and to beseech Him to send into your poor ignorant and sinful soul if but one single ray of His heavenly light. For His Divine grace is like Himself, all-powerful, so that one single ray suffices to light up the darkness of your mind, give life and activity to your will and fill you with His heavenly comfort.

Then say to Him with all earnestness and humility: Come, O Holy Spirit! send down from heaven but one ray of Thy Divine Light, that I may know what Thou wishest me to do, and be enabled to do it. Amen.

8. Second Day of the Novena

1. "*Come, Thou Father of the poor.*" These words remind you of your poverty. But are you really poor? Surely, there can be no poverty greater than yours. What are you of yourself? What have you of yourself? What can you do of yourself? The answer to each question is alike: Absolutely nothing. Of yourself, you are void of all good, natural and supernatural. Left to yourself, you can do nothing deserving the least reward, either temporal or eternal. Of yourself, you are left defenceless in the midst of your enemies, a prey to misery and wretchedness, to death and all evils—a just penalty due to sin. Left to yourself, you cannot even pray aright and call upon God to help you in your poverty and misery. Yet be not dismayed. There is One Who will be a tender, loving Father to you. It is the Holy Ghost. Hence Jesus Christ, in promising Him, had said: "I will not leave you orphans." This Divine Spirit will fill you with the heavenly riches of His Divine grace. He will take you "under the shadow of His wings, and protect you

as the apple of His eye." Yet first humbly acknowledge your poverty. Humility is truth, and you are poor in very truth.

Then turn to the Divine Spirit with sentiments of true humility, and earnestly implore Him to enrich your poverty by the riches of His Divine grace. Say to Him thus: Come, O Holy Spirit, Thou Father of the poor! Come, fill my poverty-stricken soul out of the plenty of Thy heavenly riches.

2. *"Come, Thou Giver of Gifts."* What are the gifts of the Holy Ghost? or rather, what is there, in the order of nature, or of grace, that is not His gift? All that is bright and beautiful, good and perfect, has been made so by Him. The grace and comeliness of the human body, the grandeur and nobility of the human soul, these are His gifts. The creations of man's genius in arts and sciences, are inspirations caught from the Divine Spirit. But what about the supernatural gifts of grace, virtue, holiness, and perfection? Who can enumerate them? Who can fathom them? Who can describe them? Consider the life of the ordinary Christian in his daily struggles for mastery over himself. He may fall now and again; but he rises as often. "The spirit is willing, the flesh is weak." Yes, he is weak and frail. But he is, nevertheless, in thorough earnest. His will is strong and determined. And he continues to the end, in spite of all obstacles. Now the light, strength, peace, joy and comfort he experiences

on earth, and the glory and happiness in store for him in heaven; all these are the gifts of the Holy Ghost.

Between the life of the ordinary Christian and the lives of those great Servants of God whom Holy Church has glorified, and placed upon her altars for our veneration, encouragement and imitation—what a vast range of grace and perfection, of extraordinary favors and privileges opens itself out to our view till we are lost in the dizzy heights of sublime virtue and heroic sanctity. All this is, once more, an effect of the gifts of the Holy Ghost.

If you are, therefore, still poor in grace and perfection, whose fault is it but your own? If you really desire to lead a life of virtue, and still find yourself chained down by the fetters of sin, whose fault is it but your own? The Holy Ghost offers you His Divine gifts in abundance. True, as there are not two individuals who are altogether alike, neither does the Divine Spirit deal with all men in the same manner. He accommodates His gifts to the particular needs and conditions of each individual; yet to everyone He offers more than enough.

Then, once more, approach the Divine Spirit with a humble and contrite heart, and a grateful acknowledgment of all past favors, and say with all confidence: Come, O Holy Spirit! Thou Giver of gifts! Bestow upon me out of the inexhaustible treasury of Thy Divine gifts whatever Thou knowest to be needful to me, for Thy greater honor and glory, the salvation of my own poor soul, and the welfare of my fellow-men.

3. "*Come. Thou Light of hearts.*" What would we do without light? Without light, all would be dark and dreary, cold and miserable. But with light, everything becomes lightsome and joyful. Yet what is the light of the heart? It is love. Hence it is written: "Love God, and your heart shall be enlightened;" and, again: "He that loveth his brother, abideth in the light." Love, therefore, is the light that floods the heart of man with the sunshine of peace and contentment. Yet not everything which bears the name of love is love in reality. The love which alone can fill man's heart with true joy and happiness, is that heaven-born love, "the charity of God, diffused in our hearts by the Holy Ghost." It is, once more, a special gift of the Holy Ghost, by which we are enabled to love God, for His own sake, above all things, and our neighbor as ourselves, for God's sake. When, therefore, this Divine spirit of Love and Charity personally dwells in your soul, how can it remain darksome and wretched? The Holy Ghost Himself is the Light of your heart, enkindling within you the fire of Divine love.

Then again call upon Him to abide with you: Come, O Holy Spirit! Thou Light of hearts! Set my heart all on fire with Divine love. Then shall I love as I ought, enjoy true peace and happiness, and shed abroad the same upon all with whom I shall come in contact.

9. Third Day of the Novena

1. "*O Thou Best Comforter.*" What a fearful havoc did not sin make of God's beautiful creation! What a sad spectacle does not now this earth present! How deeply has not our own human nature been wounded and degraded! Yes, there is now nothing but misery and wretchedness, pain and sorrow, and finally death with all its dread surroundings. Assuredly, we could not bear up, left to ourselves. If there were no one to look up to for comfort, nearly every one would, sooner or later, fall a prey to black despair. Yet be not faint-hearted. The Holy Ghost is your Comforter, and of all comforters the best. True, He will not set you free from your present miseries as long as you live in this valley of tears. Now you must suffer. There is no other choice left. Then bear the ills of this life patiently, out of love for God, in atonement for sin, and in union with the sufferings of your Crucified Redeemer. In this, the Holy Ghost will most certainly assist you by the might of His all-powerful grace.

Yet, you must not fail to invoke His aid. When, therefore, the cross hangs heavily upon your weak shoulders and weighs you down to the ground with its burden; when trials and afflictions overwhelm you; when grief and sadness tend your heart; when temptations endeavor to allure you away from God; aye, and when sin actually holds you enslaved and gives you to taste of its bitterness—oh! then call upon Him Who is your true and only Comforter: Come, Holy Ghost, O Thou best Comforter! Strengthen me in my weakness! Uphold me in my misery! Deliver me from sin! Comfort me in my distress! Thou art my Helper and my Protector.

2. "*Thou, the soul's sweet Guest.*" The Holy Ghost is your Comforter. But how does He comfort you? Not at a distance, or from afar, but right within your soul. Not through the instrumentality of others, or even by His gifts, but by His own Divine Presence. Yes, He personally comes to take up His abode within you. Your soul becomes His tabernacle, your very body His living temple. Do you understand what this means? When Solomon dedicated the Temple he had built, "the glory of the Lord filled the house of God" in the form of a cloud, and thus God dwelt with His chosen people. At the sight of this, Solomon cried out: "Is it credible then that God should dwell with men on the earth? If heaven, and the heavens of heavens, cannot contain Thee, how much less this house which I have built?" If Solomon was amazed at the thought that God should condescend to dwell with His people, what should not be the sentiments of wonder and admiration, aye and of love and thanksgiving, when you reflect that He "Whom the heavens of heavens cannot contain" has actually condescended to abide in your soul! And for what purpose?

To dedicate you as His living temple, to ennoble, elevate and enrich your entire being with the plenitude of His gifts, to comfort you on earth and crown you with everlasting bliss in heaven.

Yet, bear in mind, the Holy Ghost wishes to come to you as a guest. But no guest comes unbidden. He will not, therefore, come to you unless you invite Him. Then say to Him with all humility: Come, O Holy Ghost! Be Thou the sweet guest of my poor soul. Abide with me always. I thank Thee for having condescended to regard the lowliness of Thy servant. I adore Thee truly present within the tabernacle of my soul. May I never offend Thee again, but thank, praise and glorify Thee forever.

3. "*Sweet Refreshment, Thou.*" The Holy Ghost is your Comforter. He comforts you by His personal indwelling. He Himself is your soul's sweet Refreshment. Do you realize this? When you are in sorrow and distress, where do you look for comfort? Do you not, at times, turn to creatures, and forget Him Who alone can give peace to your soul? And how is it that you sometimes murmur and complain? If you would only look up to the Divine Spirit and bear in mind that He gives you Himself to comfort your soul, all things would become sweet and easy to you.

Then say again: Come, O Holy Ghost! Be Thou my soul's sweet Refreshment! Abide with me during my weary sojourn in this valley of tears. Stand by me especially when the shadows of death fall upon me. Forget me not when Divine Justice detains me for a time in the cleansing flames of Purgatory. Fan my soul, O Celestial Dove, with Thy wings so as to temper the ardor of the avenging fire, and inspire others to comfort me with their prayers. And when the fiery breath of Thy Love has consumed within my soul all earthly dross and stains of sin, then be Thou my soul's sweet Refreshment forever in the glory of Thy Heavenly Kingdom.

10. Fourth Day of the Novena

1. "*Thou art Rest in labor.*" Labor has been imposed on man from the beginning. "The Lord God took man and put him into the paradise of pleasure, to dress it, and to keep it." Then labor was an occupation of delight and enjoyment; but after the fall, it became a toilsome burden. "Cursed is the earth in Thy work... With labor and toil shalt thou eat thereof. . . . Thorns and thistles shall it bring forth. . . . In the sweat of thy face shalt thou eat bread." Labor is now a penance and a cross, and most men submit to it only through sheer necessity. Who will support you in labor, and give you rest? Behold, the Holy Ghost Himself is your Rest in labor. He enlightens your mind to understand that labor is a command imposed upon you by God, and that the fatigues, toils and worries accompanying it are now a

penalty due to sin. And in proportion as He enlightens your mind, He strengthens your will, so that you may avoid idleness, employ your time in honest and useful labor, and accept its hardships in all humble submission to God's Holy Will, without ever a murmur or complaint. The Divine Spirit will, moreover, sanctify your labor, so as to make it productive of supernatural merit and reward. If you consecrate to God your daily toil, it will obtain for you many special graces, it will satisfy for sin, lessen the temporal debt due to sin, and lay up for you a treasure in heaven. Even the material result of your labor will be blessed by God, so that you may have enough for your own daily needs, and yet be able to spare something to bestow in charity on your poorer Brethren. In this manner, the Holy Ghost is Rest in your labor here below and will be your eternal Rest hereafter in heaven. Then labor manfully and courageously in the Holy Ghost, so as to enter into His Rest.

2. "*Thou art Shelter from the heat.*" There is heat which is the result of strife and conflict. Man's life on earth is a continual warfare. You are surrounded by enemies on all sides, enemies from within, and from without. You have to contend against the evil tendencies of your corrupt nature. You have to wrestle with the spirits of darkness. You have to defend yourself against the allurements of this world. The battle is almost continual and uninterrupted. It lasts as long as life itself

will last. Your enemies are powerful. The battle is fierce. Who is to be your shelter in the heat of the battle but the Holy Ghost? He will protect you under the covert of His wings, and defend you against all your enemies, as a hen guards her little ones against the birds of prey. He will enable you to fight the good fight, and obtain the palm of victory. When temptation, therefore, lays hold on you, when the heat of the conflict seems to exhaust and oppress you, do not fail to call upon the Holy Ghost to be your shelter from the heat.

There is heat which results from the human passions. Passions, in themselves, are not sinful; on the contrary, they are useful, and even necessary. Without them, nothing great, noble or sublime would ever have been achieved by men. But human passions are blind; they must be controlled and kept in proper check; otherwise they will, like an untamed and unbridled horse, run away with you, and bring disaster upon you. But to bridle and tame the passions, and keep them in proper check, is, at times, most difficult. Experience proves it but too well. Who will assist you? Once more the Holy Ghost. By the power of His Divine Grace, He will temper the ardor and glow of your passions, subject them to the dictates of right reason, and compel them to submit to the yoke of God's Holy law.

And not infrequently has the Holy Ghost even literally been a shelter from physical heat, as we read in the acts of many holy martyrs. By a special miracle, the Holy Ghost so tempered the heat of the fire that some of them walked upon burning coals as upon a path strewn with roses, and remained unhurt in the midst of devouring flames as though taking a most refreshing bath.

When heat, therefore, oppresses you with its stifling atmosphere, call upon the Holy Ghost to come and abide within your very soul, to be your shelter from the heat.

3. *"Thou art Solace in our weeping."* There are tears which are bitter and painful. They arise from the sorrows and afflictions of this life, from the loss of temporal goods, or the departure of some one near and dear to us. Such tears are natural, and not to be condemned, provided they are kept within bounds, according to the dictates of reason and faith. Never yield to excessive and unreasonable grief. Do not weep like those that have no hope. If temporal misfortunes befall you, call upon the Holy Ghost. He is your Solace in this vale of tears.

But there are, also, tears which are sweet and consoling.

There are the tears of compunction for sin. Such tears are precious; for they touch the heart of God and wash away the stain of guilt.

There are the tears of compassion at the sorrows of your fellow-men. Such tears are noble; for they lead to heroic deeds of charity and self-sacrifice in the service of your neighbor.

There are the tears of grief and lament, arising from the consideration of Christ's bitter Passion and Death: or of the many offenses by which the Divine Majesty is constantly being outraged by men. Such tears are good and holy; for they bring you nearer to God.

There are the tears of holy joy and desire which spring from the contemplation of Divine and heavenly things. Such tears are sublime; for they raise you above all mundane affairs and give you here on earth already a foretaste of the joys of heaven.

All these kinds of tears are in themselves a special gift of the Holy Ghost. Then humbly ask the Divine Spirit to grant you this gift which of itself is an unfailing source of sweet joy and comfort in the Holy Ghost. Of such as possess this gift, it is written: "Blessed are they that mourn: for they shall be comforted."

11. Fifth Day of the Novena

"O Thou, most blissful Light! Fill the inmost hearts of Thy faithful." The sense of sight is, indeed, most precious. Without it, we should be plunged in continual darkness. The beauties of nature, and the creations of art, would be without charm or meaning. Even our other senses would, in a manner, be crippled, as they depend, in a great measure, on the sense of sight. Yet

what would sight itself be without light? Take away light, and even the keenest sight would be of no avail. All things would lie buried in impenetrable darkness. But as soon as light appears, all things are seen in their full reality, and the heart is filled with gladness at the vision of beauty spread out before its view. Light is therefore the medium in which, and by which, we behold things and rejoice at seeing them. Hence light is a most blissful thing.

Do you see God? Not directly, at present, or face to face. To gaze directly on the ravishing beauty of His Divine Countenance is the happy lot of the Blessed in heaven. But you are still on this earth. You can now only see Him, as it were, from afar, and hence very imperfectly.

Do you know God? Yes, you do know something concerning God. But this knowledge also is, at present, very limited and imperfect, on account of the manner in which you obtain this knowledge.

And yet, even the faint glimpse that you now have of God, and the little knowledge you possess of Him, comes to you in, and by, the Holy Ghost. He is your Light.

You know God both naturally and supernaturally. Naturally from the consideration of created things, and supernaturally by faith.

You look around you and you behold a certain degree of goodness and perfection in every creature. But since God made all things as they are, your very reason tells you that He must be far and away above all creatures, and must, of necessity, surpass, in an infinite degree, all creatures in goodness and perfection. Hence in the goodness and perfection of finite and created things, you catch a glimpse of the infinite goodness and perfection of God. But is not the Holy Ghost He Who completes all things and endows them with goodness and perfection? The goodness and perfection of created things are, therefore, an immediate gift of the Holy Ghost. And since in them you see God, however imperfectly, it follows that you do so in the Light of the Holy Spirit.

But you also know God supernaturally. For He has revealed Himself to man in a supernatural manner. The knowledge you thus obtain, though still imperfect, is certainly far superior to the knowledge you have of Him naturally from the consideration of creatures.

Yet how do you know God supernaturally? It is by Faith. But is not Faith a special gift of the Holy Ghost, which He Himself directly infused into your soul along with sanctifying grace at the moment of Baptism and which He perfected in the Sacrament of Confirmation? Your Faith is based upon the fact of Divine Revelation. But was it not the Holy Ghost by whom Divine Revelation has, at any time, been made known to men? He is the Author of the inspired writings. He has preserved pure and intact the Sacred Truths that have been handed down to us by Divine Tradition.

Divine Revelation was completed by Jesus Christ and His Apostles. But has not Jesus Christ Himself been given to you by the Holy Ghost? And did not the Holy Ghost come down upon the Apostles in a special manner, as the Spirit of Truth, to teach them all things?

Divine Revelation is inviolably guarded and infallibly communicated to men by the living voice of the Church of Jesus Christ. But to whom does the Church owe her existence? Who makes her infallible? Who keeps her from even the least shadow of error? Who communicates to the Sovereign Pontiff, the Head of God's True Church, the gift of personal infallibility, so that he may safely feed the lambs and the sheep entrusted to his keeping by the Divine Shepherd? It is the Holy Ghost.

Thus you perceive that, in the supernatural order of things, it is, likewise, the Holy Ghost, in Whom, and by Whom you know God.

And what is meant by that beatific Vision, or happy-making sight, by which the Blessed see God in heaven and are happy with Him for ever? It means this, that in heaven the Holy Ghost will communicate Himself to your soul in so full and complete a measure that He Himself will be the very Light of your soul, in which and by which, you will see God face to face in all His glorious

Reality, take full possession of Him, and enjoy Him for all eternity in unspeakable joy and happiness. The Holy Ghost will thus be the most blissful Light, in which, and by which, you shall enjoy the sight of God forever.

In this manner the Divine Spirit is the Light by which you now come to know God, in order to love and serve Him on earth; and having been led by Him to the knowledge of God now, He will hereafter be the Light leading you to the Beatific Vision. Hence it is written: "The light of Thy countenance, O Lord, is signed upon us: Thou hast given gladness in my heart . . . For with Thee is the Fountain of Life, and in Thy Light we shall see Light."

Then call upon the Divine Spirit to be your Light. Pray to Him, likewise, on behalf of all men. Say to Him with all fervor and devotion: Come, O Holy Spirit! O Thou, most blissful Light! Come and fill the inmost hearts of Thy faithful, that they may rejoice in Thy Light, now and forever more.

12. Sixth Day of the Novena

1. "*Unless Thou givest, there is naught in man, naught but what is sinful.*" Since every gift of nature and of grace, that ever has been, can, or will be, bestowed upon you, proceeds from the Divine Spirit, it follows that, without Him, you are nothing; or if you wish to claim anything as your own, it is your sins and miseries. In so far as

God made you, you were made aright and filled with every blessing. If, therefore, you are now subject to sin and misery, this is your handiwork. Then, once more, humbly acknowledge your own nothingness and sinfulness, and your utter dependence on the Holy Ghost, and say to Him again with all fervor and devotion: Come, O Holy Spirit! Be Thou my Assistance; for without Thee, I am nothing but sin and misery.

2. *"Wash Thou what is stained."* It is sin which defiles the human soul. Original sin has, like a universal deluge, swept over the whole human race and now causes each soul that is born into this world to come into existence without that supernatural beauty and perfection which God had bestowed upon man in the beginning. Actual sin adds to that original defilement, or, once more, disfigures the soul after it had been adorned with Divine grace. Mortal sin blots out entirely that supernatural beauty and perfection with which a soul is endowed when in the state of grace. Venial sin soils and stains the white garment of sanctifying grace.

Who cleanses your soul from sin? It is the Holy Ghost. For He applies to you the infinite merits of your Divine Redeemer, and washes, so to speak, your soul in the Blood of Jesus Christ.

Are you in sin? Oh! delay not to call upon the Divine Spirit. Diligently employ the means of pardon and reconciliation, and then pray to Him and fervently say:

Come, O Holy Spirit! Cleanse my sinful soul from all
stain and guilt of sin. Wash me yet more from my iniquity, and cleanse me from my sin. Wash me, and I shall
be made whiter than snow.

3. "*Water what is parched.*" Look around you on
a hot summer's day. All nature is languid. Vegetation
seems to be withered and dried up. The soil is furrowed
with deep cracks. What is amiss? The earth is parched
and thirsts for rain. Such is the state of a soul that suf-
fers from dryness and aridity. All spiritual activity seems
to have died out. The soul finds no relish in doing what
is right. It has, in fact, almost become barren of every
good. What is needed? The vivifying and refreshing
showers of Divine grace. Yet why does the Holy Ghost,
that Heavenly Cloud, withhold, at times, the outpouring of His grace, and leaves your soul parched and withered? It is chiefly because you have grown careless and
neglectful in prayer. You pray but seldom; and when
you pray you do so in a listless manner. There is no heart
in it. You hardly know yourself what you are about.
Surely, that is not prayer. No wonder that your prayers
are not answered. No wonder that your soul becomes
"like earth that is without water."

Yet bear in mind that even prayer itself is a special
gift of the Holy Ghost; for, without Him you cannot
pray aright, or even know what you should ask for in
prayer.

Then rouse yourself, and, with all the intensity of your being, call upon the Divine Spirit to grant you the gift and the spirit of prayer, so that you may pray, on all occasions, in a manner pleasing to God. Such prayer will pierce the Cloud and draw down upon you the refreshing showers of heavenly grace. Then will your soul be clothed with verdure and bring forth an abundance of good fruit in due season.

4. *"Heal Thou what is wounded."* Original sin inflicted a deep wound on the human soul. The mind was darkened, the will enfeebled and enslaved, all power for good impaired, and human nature rendered prone to evil. By your own actual sins, you make the case still worse; for you add wound upon wound. Your Divine Savior is the Good Samaritan that took compassion upon you. He bound up your wounds, pouring in oil and wine, and carried you to the Inn to be taken care of and nursed. Yes, the Church of Christ is the Divine Sanitarium where you will find an infallible remedy for all the wounds and ailments of your soul. The priests of God's Church are the legitimate Physicians authorized by God to probe your wounds and apply the remedies. The Word of God and the Divine Sacraments are the remedies they employ. But who is it that actually applies to your soul internally the soothing and healing balm of Divine Grace? This is the Holy Ghost. Then do your best to make use of all the means prepared for you by

your Divine Samaritan; but do not fail, at the same time, to call upon the Holy Ghost, the Divine Physician of your soul, and say to Him: Come O Holy Spirit! Thou heavenly Physician of my poor soul! Heal Thou the wounds inflicted on my soul by sin, that it may be strengthened, and live only for God.

13. Seventh Day of the Novena

1. *"Bend Thou what is rigid."* Sin darkens the mind, hardens the heart, and renders the will stiff and stubborn so as to refuse to submit to God's holy will and yield to the guidance of His Divine Spirit. Obstinacy is, therefore, a common ingredient of every sin. But obstinacy sometimes reaches such a degree as to constitute a special sin. Of this sin the Jews as a nation were guilty in a particular manner, which made St. Stephen say to them: "With a stiff neck and uncircumcised heart and ears, you always resist the Holy Ghost. As your fathers did, so do you also." This sin of obstinacy is usually fatal; for it is one of the sins directly opposed to the Holy Ghost.

Are you stubborn and obstinate? You may not have gone quite so far as to resist the Holy Ghost entirely. But are there not a number of small infidelities of which you are guilty, almost every day, though small they should not be called; for it is no small matter to resist the Holy Ghost, and you do resist Him each time you fall into deliberate venial sins.

Are you not stubborn and obstinate, when you refuse to correct certain faults and when you are displeased at being reprimanded even by those who have a right to do so? Does not this clearly show that your heart is still attached to sin?

Are you not stubborn and obstinate when you display a certain coldness and harshness in the intercourse with your fellowmen, when you refuse to be reconciled to them, when you are hard and over-exacting with regard to those who owe you anything?

Examine yourself well and do not refuse to acknowledge that, in many ways, your will has become stubborn and obstinate. Then beg and implore the Divine Spirit to render your will pliable to the influence of His Divine grace. Ask Him to give you the grace so to hate sin as to avoid every deliberate venial sin and correct yourself of your failings and shortcomings. Ask Him to make you docile and obedient so as to put no obstacles to the workings of His Divine grace, but always follow His inspirations. Ask Him to make you meek and humble, kind and gentle, loving and forgiving. Thus will the Holy Ghost bend in your regard that which is rigid and render it yielding to His loving influence.

2. "*Warm Thou what is cold.*" Selfishness is a dangerous and insidious vice; and yet, like obstinacy, it enters, in some degree or other, into every sin. He who is selfish,

thinks only of himself, loves only himself, works only
for himself, and since all his motives are concentrated
upon self, there is no room left either for God or for
his fellow-men. Selfishness, therefore, dries up the very
root and source of true charity which is the love of God
and of one's neighbor. And is not every sin opposed to
charity? But selfishness also becomes at times a special
sin, and a sin which unfortunately is not uncommon.

But what is the effect of selfishness upon the human
heart? Love enlarges the heart and renders it sensible
to the claims of God and man. Selfishness narrows the
heart and makes it insensible to divine and human
claims. Love sets the heart all on fire and makes its
gentle influence to be felt all around. Selfishness dries
up all gentle feelings, makes the heart cold, and dif-
fuses an atmosphere of icy chill. Love brings with it its
own reward, for it fills the heart with joy and gladness.
Selfishness brings in its train its own punishment; for
it causes misery and wretchedness. Love is the very life
of the human heart. Selfishness is its death. In fact the
selfish are said to have no heart.

Are you not selfish in many ways? When will you
cease to be so? Call upon the Divine Spirit of Love to
breathe upon your cold heart and to melt that icy crust
of selfishness. Thus will He warm that which is cold and
make you aglow with the fire of His own Divine Love.

3. *"Guide Thou what is erring."* Sin causes man to turn aside from God and turn to creatures. The sinner forgets that God alone is his true end and destiny, and fixes all his attention upon creatures as though he were made for them. He loses sight of heaven, his true home, and attaches himself to the things of this earth, as though he were to live forever on this earth. He becomes indifferent about the eternal interests of his immortal soul and labors only for the perishable goods of this world. All such have gone astray altogether.

You may not have turned aside from God entirely, and yet be as an erring sheep that has gone astray. To allow too much liberty to your thoughts and desires, not to keep a proper check on your imaginations and passions, not to watch sufficiently over your senses and appetites, to think too much of the necessities of your perishable body, to be engrossed too much with the cares of this world, to allow your heart to be attached to trifles: all this turns you aside, distracts you and hinders your progress on the way to heaven.

Then pray to the Divine Spirit to lead you into the right path that leads straight to your heavenly country. Ask Him for the grace to have your eyes always fixed on God, your first beginning and last end, and to do all your actions with a pure motive of pleasing God and saving your immortal soul.

Be guided in all things by the Holy Ghost. Devotedly obey God's Holy Church and faithfully submit to all lawful authority. Thus He guides externally. Be careful to heed and obey the inspirations of Divine grace, by which He guides you internally. Thus the Divine Spirit will guide in you that which is erring. And if He be your Guide, you will never stray from the right path, but infallibly reach your final end and destiny.

14. Eighth Day of the Novena

"*Give unto Thy faithful, who put their trust in Thee, Thy most sacred sevenfold gift.*" Along with sanctifying grace, the Holy Ghost infuses into your soul the three theological Virtues: Faith, Hope, and Charity, and the germ of every other virtue, especially of the four great Cardinal Virtues: Prudence, Justice, Fortitude, and Temperance. Now the Seven Gifts of the Holy Ghost are bestowed upon you in order to assist you in the practice of these seven important virtues. It is thus the Divine Spirit places you wholly under His guidance and makes you capable of performing the most sublime and heroic deeds of virtue and perfection, and reach an eminent degree of holiness.

The gift of Understanding endows you with a keen insight into the hidden meaning of the revealed Truths of Religion, and thereby assists you in the practice of the Virtue of Faith.

The gift of Knowledge shows you how to set a right value on all things as viewed in the light of Divine Revelations and thereby assists you in the practice of the Virtue of Hope.

The gift of Wisdom places all things before you in their relation to God, their first beginning and last end, and in relation to each other, and thereby assists you in the practice of the Virtue of Charity.

The gift of Counsel shows you what to do or to avoid under particular circumstances, and thereby assists you in the practice of the Virtue of Prudence.

The gift of Piety moves you to give to God that filial love and service you owe Him as to your heavenly Father and respect each other as members of that universal Family of which God is the Father, and thereby assists you in the practice of the Virtue of Justice which inclines the Will to give everyone his due.

The gift of Fortitude imparts you special strength to overcome all difficulties in the practice of virtue, and thereby assists you in the practice of the Virtue of Fortitude.

The gift of the Fear of the Lord, by making you sensible of your own nothingness as compared to the infinite majesty of God, keeps you in your right place, moderates your passions and desires, and thereby assists you in the practice of the Virtue of Temperance.

Do you realize what all this means? Oh, how can you
ever sufficiently thank the Divine Spirit for all the aid
He is constantly giving you.

You were born a slave to sin and misery. The Holy
Ghost washed away sin, raised you to the dignity of
the sonship of God and gave you a right to the eternal inheritance of heaven. But what can you do towards
the attainment of heaven, if left to yourself, and yet you
must do something. Hence the Holy Ghost Himself
enables you to believe in God, to hope in Him, and to
love Him above everything, and likewise to acquire and
to practice every other virtue. But the practice of virtue
also is, at times, very difficult, and even painful to poor
human nature. This obstacle has likewise been removed
by the Divine Spirit by bestowing upon you seven special gifts which will render the practice of virtue sweet
and easy. If with all this Divine Assistance, you fail to
lead a good and virtuous life and reach heaven hereafter,
surely the fault can only be your own.

Yet you must ever bear in mind that if you actually
wish to possess these Seven Gifts of the Holy Ghost,
you must implore Him by humble and fervent prayer to
bestow them upon you and enable you to use them. It
is in the Sacrament of Confirmation that He grants you
these Seven Gifts in a special manner. For it is then He
strengthens within you the life of grace so as to practice
virtue in spite of all obstacles. But even then He will give

them only in proportion to the fervor and earnestness of the prayers with which you beseech Him to come to you. Yet at other times also you must pray to Him for these Gifts; in fact you should do so continually, for you need them continually. And the Holy Ghost bestows upon you afresh His Divine Gifts each time you need them, and ask for them by humble prayer.

But here you are reminded to pray not merely for yourself individually, but for all the faithful of the Holy Ghost, who put their trust in Him. "Grant unto Thy faithful who put their trust in Thee, Thy most Sacred Sevenfold Gift." Who are the faithful of the Holy Ghost? Those whom He filled with faith in the Sacrament of Baptism. Hence you should pray first on behalf of all the members of God's Church that the Holy Ghost who imbued them with faith, would please to complete His work in them by granting them His Seven Gifts which will enable them to practice and profess their faith openly in spite of all opposition and contradiction. And among the faithful you pray for those in a special manner who have placed all their confidence in the Power of the Divine Spirit.

But while praying for those who already belong to the true Faith, surely you will not forget to pray for those also who are still deprived of the inestimable blessings of God's true Faith.

Then pray to the Holy Ghost and say to Him: Come,

O Holy Ghost, fill the whole earth and lead all men to the knowledge of the one true Faith.

Come, O Holy Ghost, and fill Thou the hearts of Thy faithful. Without Thee, we can do nothing. In Thee do we put all our trust. Give unto us Thy most Sacred Sevenfold Gift. Give us the spirit of understanding that we may believe in Thee more firmly. Give us the spirit of Knowledge that we may hope in Thee more confidently. Give us the spirit of Wisdom that we may love Thee more ardently. Give us the spirit of Counsel that we may be more prudent in all our actions. Give us the spirit of Piety that we may be more just in all our dealings in regard to God and to men. Give us the spirit of Fortitude that we may be able to overcome more easily all obstacles in the way of virtue. Give us the spirit of the Fear of the Lord, that we may be more moderate in all things. Thus assist us all continually, O Divine Spirit, by Thy sevenfold Gift, that we may glorify Thee on earth by a good and virtuous life and be glorified by Thee in the kingdom of heaven.

15. Ninth Day of the Novena

1. *"Give Thou virtue its reward."* Virtues are but as a means to the end. It is by the practice of virtue, that you become virtuous, are made fruitful in every good work and pleasing in God's sight, and merit for yourself an increase of grace on earth and of glory in heaven.

Virtues are therefore, the seeds; good works, deserving of everlasting life, the fruits thereof. But is it not the Holy Ghost Who implants every virtue in your soul, and renders its practice sweet and easy? And if thus the Holy Ghost is the primary author of virtue, then the fruit of virtue must, likewise, be ascribed to Him. He it is, therefore, Who makes you good and virtuous, and renders you fruitful in every good work and pleasing in God's sight. He it is that rewards your soul now all ready with an increase of holiness and perfection and an assurance of an eternal recompense in heaven. Thus the reward of virtue is, likewise, a special gift of the Holy Ghost. Let this consideration be another motive of returning sincere thanks to the Divine Spirit for all He is doing for you. Let it also be a motive of keeping you in true humility. For even if you reached the very pinnacle of sanctity, and were favored like St. Paul to be rapt up into the third heaven, and to see and hear things it is not given to men to see and hear, it would be sinful for you to glory in any such thing as though it were your own work entirely, but you should be truthful in saying with the same Saint: "For myself, I will glory in nothing but in my infirmities."

Then humbly acknowledge all this and say with all sincerity: O Divine Spirit of holiness and perfection, Who hast been pleased to beautify my soul with the gift of every virtue and hast rendered its practice sweet and easy, I humbly beseech Thee: Do Thou, likewise, complete the work Thou hast wrought in me, and bestow upon me the sweet reward of virtue in time and in eternity.

2. *"Grant a happy end."* To begin well is good; to continue in well-doing, is better; but to persevere in grace and virtue to the end, is best. Hence the Divine Spirit Himself declares: "He that shall persevere to the end, the same shall be saved;" and again: "To him that persevereth I will give the crown of life." A happy end and a holy death is, therefore, the most important thing. Yes, precious in the sight of God is the death of His saints." But who will enable you to persevere unto the end and to die a good and a happy death? None other but the Divine Spirit. Final Perseverance is, indeed, one of the special graces of the Holy Ghost, and of all graces, the most important and essential in your regard. If, therefore, you earnestly desire to secure a happy end, you must, once more, have recourse to prayer. And you may rest assured that if you persevere in daily praying for the grace of a happy death, you will infallibly persevere in all good to the end, and die a good and happy death.

Then say to the Holy Ghost with all fervor and earnestness: Never depart from me, O Divine Spirit, but stay with me all the days of my life. Be Thou with me especially at the moment of my death. Oh! grant unto me the grace of perseverance to the end, that I may live and die in Thy grace and friendship and remain forever united to Thee in Thy heavenly glory.

3. *"Grant eternal happiness."* If, by the grace of the Holy Ghost, you persevere unto the end, and die a good and happy death, you will undoubtedly enter into eternal happiness. Your soul may be detained for a while in Purgatory, to be thoroughly cleansed from every stain of sin and rendered fit to appear in God's most holy sight. But when the debt due to Divine Justice has been fully paid, your soul will at once be admitted into the everlasting joys of heaven. And this will be the crowning gift of the Holy Ghost. Through Him you are now helped and assisted in every possible way to lead a good life and die a holy death. Through Him, therefore, the joys and glory of heaven will, likewise, be communicated to you. He is the Light, in which, and through which, you shall see the Uncreated, Eternal Light, God Himself, face to face. He is the Link that will then unite you forever to God, so as never again to be separated from Him. In Him, you will then wholly be made one with God so as to partake of God's own Life, Glory, and Happiness forevermore. For He who is the Love of the Father and of the Son, will then fully communicate Himself to you, so that the Uncreated Love of the Godhead will permeate every nerve and fiber of your entire being. Being plunged in that infinite ocean of God's Eternal Love, you will then fully realize God's infinite Love in your regard,

and then will you, too, fully love God with all the energy of your whole being. Then will you, moreover meet in loving embrace and fond intercourse with the countless choirs of bright, angelic Spirits, and the vast array of the saints and Blessed of God, and with those also who were near and dear to you on earth and from whom you were parted but for a time, and the Holy Ghost Himself will be that boundless Ocean of Infinite Love, uniting all to God, and God to all, and each to each other, in everlasting bliss and glory, causing each soul to thrill through and through with ecstasies of joy and happiness unutterable. Poor, indeed, is all human language to convey even the least idea of the glory and happiness of heaven. For "eye hath not seen, nor ear heard, neither hath it entered into the heart of man to conceive what God hath prepared for them that love Him."

But what of your body? Is it to be overlooked? Is not your body part of yourself, taking now its own share in the burdensome toils of this mortal life? Has not your body, likewise, been sanctified? Is it not the living temple of the Holy Ghost? And shall that living temple of His be a prey to death forever? Certainly not. True, it must die and return to the earth from which it came. For "dust thou art, and unto dust thou shall return." Such is the just sentence of God upon all mankind on account of sin. But your body shall not remain in the tomb forever; it shall rise again, and "in this very flesh you shall see your Savior," and be united to God forever. And the resurrection of your body at the last day is, likewise, the special work of the Holy Ghost, the Life-giver. At that day the Spirit of God will breathe upon the face of the earth: and, in the twinkling of an eye, the bodies of the dead will be quickened into life again, and endowed with perpetual youth and immortality. Then, if you are of the number of the elect, your body will not only be raised to life again, but will also be glorified, and made altogether alike to the risen body of Christ. Your body will then shine more brilliantly than the sun, move from place to place more swiftly than the flash of lightning, be able to pass through massive rocks more easily than the light entering through glass, and be adorned with beauty and immortality forever. Then will your body, too, have its share in the pleasures and delights of the heavenly Paradise. Thus will you then live forever in the sunshine of God's own Love for all ages to come.

If now sometimes this exile here below appears too long and wearisome, if now sometimes the miseries of this life seem to press too heavily upon you, then lift up your head and catch a glimpse of that eternal glory and happiness which awaits you on high, prepared for you already by the Divine Spirit of Love. It will cheer you, buoy you up with hope, and enable you to bear the ills of this life patiently, till the Spirit shall release you from this exile and conduct you to your Father's home.

Yet pray. Pray most earnestly. Pray without ceasing. Come, O Divine Spirit! Come, and abide with me. Take up Thy abode in my soul and body, so that, in soul and body, I shall ever be united to Thee and in Thee, to God, my first beginning, and my last end, so that when I die I may die in union with Thee and be crowned by Thee with eternal happiness. Yea, O most loving Spirit! Love of the Father and of the Son, grant unto me, Thy most unworthy servant, when life is over, eternal happiness in heaven.

Amen. So be it. Alleluia. Praised be God for ever more.

XVII. The Seven Gifts and the Twelve Fruits of the Holy Ghost

1. Notice

In the plan of working out our eternal salvation all things needful are most bountifully provided for by God and most beautifully linked together.

Heaven is promised under a twofold title as an inheritance, and as a reward.

They who are baptized and die before they reach the years of discretion, enter heaven forthwith and take possession of it as their fatherly inheritance. But as soon as a man becomes responsible for his own acts, the former title alone will not suffice. He must also do something on his part to merit heaven as a recompense.

The first condition in either case is life, the life of sanctifying grace, infused into the soul by the Holy Ghost at Baptism.

But life in itself is not sufficient. Certain faculties or powers enabling us to act must be added. These are the supernatural habits of Faith, Hope, and Charity, and of every other virtue. These habits are, likewise, infused into the soul, along with sanctifying grace, by the Holy Ghost.

Yet the practice of virtue is impossible on our part without the special assistance of the Holy Ghost. He renders its practice *possible* by the aid of His actual grace.

But virtue, even when possible, is at times difficult. The Holy Ghost renders its practice *sweet and easy* by His Seven Gifts which He bestows in the Sacrament of Confirmation.

When, at last, with the aid of the Holy Ghost, we practice virtue, we shall produce good works which will merit for us heaven. Good works are the fruit of our virtuous actions and are rightly called the fruit of the Divine Spirit, without Whom we could not have produced them. St. Paul enumerates twelve fruits of the Spirit. These twelve fruits are intimately connected with the seven gifts.

2. Wisdom

Charity

The gift of Wisdom places all things before you in their relation to God, their first beginning and last end, and in relation to each other; and thus produces within you the fruit of Charity, the true love of God and your neighbor.

Invocation:

Spirit of Wisdom, preside over all my thoughts, words, and actions, so that, in all things, I may love God, for His own sake, above all things, and my neighbor, as myself, for God's sake.

Holy Mary, Seat of Wisdom, pray for us.

St. Ignatius, pray for us.

Our Father. Hail Mary. Glory be.

3. Understanding

Peace

The gift of Understanding endows you with a keen insight into the hidden meaning of the revealed truths of Religion, and thus sets your mind at rest, and establishes you in Peace.

Invocation:

Spirit of Understanding, do Thou teach and enlighten me, so that I may never waver in my faith, but enjoy true peace of mind and heart.

Holy Mary, Virgin most Faithful, pray for us.
St. Benedict, pray for us.
Our Father. Hail Mary. Glory be.

4. Knowledge

Joy

The gift of Knowledge shows you how to set a right value on all things as viewed in the light of Divine Revelation, and thus frees you from all cares and anxieties and produces within you spiritual Joy.

Invocation:

Spirit of Knowledge, teach me how to took at things in their true light, so that I may not be kept bound by any undue attachment to earthly matters, but ever rejoice in Thy heavenly comforts.

Holy Mary, Cause of our Joy, pray for us.
St. Augustine, pray for us.
Our Father. Hail Mary. Glory be.

5. Counsel

Benignity—Goodness

The gift of Counsel shows you what to do or to avoid, under particular circumstances; and, therefore, moves you to be kind and considerate, and ready to do good to all with whom you may come in contact, and thus produces the fruit of Benignity and Goodness.

Invocation:

Spirit of Counsel, lead me into the ways of prudence so that, on all occasions, I may do the right thing, and show myself discreet, yet withal loving and obliging, in the daily intercourse with my fellow-men.

Holy Mary, Virgin most Prudent, pray for us.
St. Alphonsus Ligouri, pray for us.
Our Father. Hail Mary. Glory be.

6. Fortitude

Patience—Longanimity

The Gift of Fortitude imparts you special strength to overcome all difficulties in the practice of virtue, renders you patient and long suffering, and thus produces the fruit of Patience and Longanimity.

Invocation:

Spirit of Fortitude, strengthen Thou my weakness so that I may not be discouraged by any obstacle in the path of virtue, but humbly and willingly submit to the crosses and trials of this life.

Holy Mary, Queen of Martyrs, pray for us.
St. Laurence, pray for us.
Our Father. Hail Mary. Glory be.

7. Piety

Faith—Mildness

The gift of Piety moves you to give to God that filial love and service you owe to God as to your heavenly Father and likewise respect each other as members of that universal Family of which God is the Father, thus filling you with all confidence towards God and sweetness towards your neighbor.

Invocation:

Spirit of Piety, implant in my heart a filial love and affection towards God, my heavenly Father, and a brotherly charity towards all men so that I may truly delight in the service of God and of my fellow-men.

Holy Mary, our Mother, pray for us.

St. Francis, pray for us.

Our Father. Hail Mary. Glory be.

8. Fear of the Lord

Modesty—Continency—Chastity

The gift of the Fear of the Lord makes you sensible of your own nothingness as compared to the infinite Majesty of God, keeps you in the right place, moderates all your desires and appetites, and thus begets within you Modesty, Continency, and Chastity.

Invocation:

Spirit of Holy Fear, restrain me from all evil, so that I may serve God with a clean heart and a chaste body.

Holy Mary, Spouse of the Holy Ghost, pray for us.

St. Dominic, pray for us.

Our Father. Hail Mary. Glory be.

XVIII. Seven Special Promises from Holy Writ

1. Notice

Numerous, if not countless, are the favors and blessings held out in Sacred Scripture to those who are under the sweet Power and loving Guidance of the Divine Spirit. The following seven promises are proposed to you in a special manner, so that you may meditate upon them, from time to time, and render due thanks, love, and adoration to the Holy Ghost for the unspeakable proofs of His most tender love and mercy.

2. Divine Adoption

"You have not received the spirit of bondage again in fear, but you have received the Spirit of Adoption of Sons, whereby we cry: Abba (Father)." (*Rom.* 8:15.)

3. Divine Endowment

"The Spirit of the Lord shall rest upon him: the Spirit

of Wisdom and Understanding, the Spirit of Counsel and of Fortitude, the Spirit of Knowledge and of Godliness, and he shall be filled with the Spirit of the Fear of the Lord." (*Isaias* 11:2–3.)

4. Participation in the Spirit of Jesus Christ

"You are not in the flesh, but in the Spirit, if so be the Spirit of God dwell in you. If any man have not the Spirit of Christ, he is none of His." (*Rom.* 8:9.)

5. Gift of Prayer

"I will pour out upon the house of David and upon the inhabitants of Jerusalem the Spirit of grace and of prayer; and they shall look upon Me Whom they have pierced." (*Zach.* 12:10.)

6. Strength to do God's Holy Will

"I will put My Spirit in the midst of you; and I will cause you to walk in the way of My commandments, and keep My judgments, and do them." (*Ezechial* 37:27.)

7. Fruit of the Spirit

"Charity, joy, peace, patience, benignity, goodness; longanimity, mildness, faith, modesty, continency, chastity." (*Galat.* 5:22–23.)

8. Life Everlasting

"He that soweth in his flesh, of the flesh also shall reap corruption; but he that soweth in the Spirit, of the Spirit shall reap Life everlasting." (*Galat.* 6:8.)

XIX. Practices Suggested

If you wish to be numbered among the true servants of the Holy Ghost, you must, above all things, show your love for Him by endeavoring, as much as you can, by the aid of His Divine grace, to avoid all deliberate sin, and to practice the virtues demanded by your state in life; for He is the Spirit of Holiness, and the Sanctifier of your soul.

But this will not suffice. You must also offer Him special tokens of your loving homage by performing some devout exercises in His honor.

Take notice, however, not to overburden yourself on this point, nor to tie yourself down too slavishly to the devotions you have chosen; still, on the other hand, do not allow yourself to be guided merely by your whims and fancies, but having selected certain devotional practices, adhere to them as faithfully as you can.

The following suggestions are offered you for your guidance:

Each day, recite some little prayer in honor of God the Holy Ghost: the daily consecration; some hymn or invocation; one of the exercises for each day in the week: the chaplet of the Holy Ghost, or a part of it; the Little Office; the Litany; or any other prayer.

Once a week, or *once a month,* choose some particular day during which you will devote some extra time to honor the Divine Spirit. Receive Holy Communion in His honor; this you might do once a week for seven consecutive weeks, or once a month for seven consecutive months. In like manner, hear Mass, or have holy Mass offered up, in honor of the Holy Ghost. Recite the Divine Office, or part of it. Read, and meditate upon, something concerning the Holy Ghost. Choose one of the seven gifts, or twelve fruits, of the Holy Ghost, or any other particular virtue to cultivate during that week or that month and take special notice of success or failure.

Once a year, sanctify Whitsun-tide in a special manner. Prepare for the great Festival of Pentecost by a Novena, or spiritual Retreat. Recite the Divine Office, or part of it, or any other suitable prayer, each day during Whitsun-week. Remember, very special indulgences are attached to the devotional exercises performed during that particular time.

During the course of your life, there are *numerous occasions* on which you should have recourse to the Holy Ghost in a special manner.

When temptation lays hold on you, when some great sorrow or affliction visits you, when serious doubts and anxieties disturb you: do not fail to call upon Him for special light and assistance.

When you are about to receive the Sacraments of Penance and Holy Communion, or assist at Mass, direct your attention to the Holy Ghost in a special manner, since He is intimately connected with these great mysteries.

But above all, when you are deliberating upon choosing your particular station in life, especially if you feel that He Himself is calling you to some higher and more perfect mode of life, in the priesthood, or the Religious State, then pray to Him long and fervently, that you may know and do His Most Holy Will.

Whenever you are about to engage upon some particular undertaking, whether spiritual or temporal, especially if it be a matter of importance, recommend its success to the Holy Ghost by special prayers. Holy Church, in her ritual, prescribes the solemn invocation of the Holy Ghost on all important occasions. In many Schools and Colleges, the Votive Mass of the Holy Ghost, or special prayers, are offered up at the beginning of the School-year.

If you have not yet received the Sacrament of Confirmation, do not fail to do so, when the first opportunity presents itself. Prepare for it with the greatest care and diligence. Live up to the solemn duties it imposes upon you. Keep its anniversary-day.

Priests and Religious, in particular, on account of the dignity of their calling, and the special duties of their state, will find many occasions on which they should have recourse to the Holy Ghost in a special manner. The same applies to those who are engaged in study or teaching.

It has not been deemed necessary to specify the particular indulgences attached to the various exercises which are here offered to the devotion of the faithful. Yet why trouble about this matter? The desire of pleasing and glorifying the Divine Spirit should be enough. Yet not to lose the benefit of the indulgences either for yourself or the suffering souls in Purgatory, make an intention, at the beginning of each day, to gain all the indulgences you can during that day. This suffices.

"Be thou faithful unto death; and I will give thee the crown of life."

XX. PIOUS UNION IN HONOR OF GOD THE HOLY GHOST

The Holy Ghost deserves to be honored in a special manner by all men, not only individually, but also in a body. It would, therefore, be a most desirable thing to see men bind themselves together for the express purpose of promoting devotion to the Holy Ghost. To this end, an association has been established, in the diocese of Indianapolis, with the sanction and approval of the Bishop under the title of *"Pious Union in honor of God the Holy Ghost."*

It has been devised upon the simplest plan. No conditions of any kind are required beyond the earnest desire of promoting devotion to the Holy Ghost. No obligations are contracted except the promise to practice special devotion to the Holy Ghost and promote the same among others. No particular form of enrollment is prescribed. Each member enrolls himself by consecrating himself to the special service of the Holy Ghost and engaging himself to do all he can towards the greater honor and glory of the Divine Spirit.

It is true, that no particular spiritual advantages are held out as inducements to join the Pious Union, beyond the Indulgences which have already been attached to the various exercises of devotion practiced in His honor. If the members reflect, in whose special service they are engaged, they will rest satisfied with the assurance, that He Whose honor and glory they are trying to promote, will amply reward them in time and in eternity.

A suitable badge has been designed and executed to express in a special manner the end of the Union. It represents the Holy Ghost in the form of a Dove with outstretched wings hovering within a triangular space from which rays dart forth all around. It shows the Holy Ghost descending from the Bosom of the Godhead to bring peace and blessings to men here below. Seven tongues of fire express His seven gifts, and twelve stars His twelve fruits. The Dove is seen hovering above the tiara and the papal arms, which represent the Church, and, in a special manner, the Sovereign Pontiff. For it is through the Church, and especially its Head, the Pope, that the Holy Ghost speaks and operates. The papal arms uphold an open Bible and a Chalice with the Sacred Host. Here we have the Holy Scriptures, the written Word of God, inspired by the Holy Ghost, and the Eternal Word of God, made Flesh, hidden under the lowly forms of the bread and wine in the Holy Eucharist, likewise brought about by the operation of the Holy Ghost. Sacred Scripture and the Holy Eucharist are indeed the chief outward manifestations of the Divine operations of the Holy Ghost, and both are confided to the safe-keeping of the Church, the very life and soul of which is the Holy Ghost. Underneath is the invocation: "Come, Holy Ghost! fill the hearts of Thy faithful; kindle in them the fire of Thy love."

Several copies of this Badge were presented at a special audience, May 13th, 1899, to His Holiness, Pope Leo XIII, who blessed them with his own hands and by word of mouth, sanctioned and approved the design.

In Conclusion

To the most holy and undivided Trinity
Father, Son and Holy Ghost
To the sacred humanity of
Our Lord, Jesus Christ Crucified
To the fruitful virginity of the
Most Blessed and Most Glorious Mary
Ever Virgin
And to the Whole Company of the Saints
Be everlasting praise, honor and glory by all creatures
world without end
Amen

Spread the Faith with . . .

TAN·BOOKS
A Division of Saint Benedict Press, LLC

TAN books are powerful tools for evangelization. They lift the mind to God and change lives. Millions of readers have found in TAN books and booklets an effective way to teach and defend the Faith, soften hearts, and grow in prayer and holiness of life.

Throughout history the faithful have distributed Catholic literature and sacramentals to save souls. St. Francis de Sales passed out his own pamphlets to win back those who had abandoned the Faith. Countless others have distributed the Miraculous Medal to prompt conversions and inspire deeper devotion to God. Our customers use TAN books in that same spirit.

If you have been helped by this or another TAN title, share it with others. Become a TAN Missionary and share our life changing books and booklets with your family, friends and community. We'll help by providing special discounts for books and booklets purchased in quantity for purposes of evangelization. Write or call us for additional details.

TAN Books
Attn: TAN Missionaries Department
P.O. Box 410487
Charlotte, NC 28241

Toll-free (800) 437-5876
missionaries@TANBooks.com

TAN·BOOKS

TAN Books was founded in 1967 to preserve the spiritual, intellectual and liturgical traditions of the Catholic Church. At a critical moment in history TAN kept alive the great classics of the Faith and drew many to the Church. In 2008 TAN was acquired by Saint Benedict Press. Today TAN continues its mission to a new generation of readers.

From its earliest days TAN has published a range of booklets that teach and defend the Faith. Through partnerships with organizations, apostolates, and mission-minded individuals, well over 10 million TAN booklets have been distributed.

More recently, TAN has expanded its publishing with the launch of Catholic calendars and daily planners—as well as Bibles, fiction, and multimedia products through its sister imprints Catholic Courses (CatholicCourses.com) and Saint Benedict Press (SaintBenedictPress.com).

Today TAN publishes over 500 titles in the areas of theology, prayer, devotions, doctrine, Church history, and the lives of the saints. TAN books are published in multiple languages and found throughout the world in schools, parishes, bookstores and homes.

**For a free catalog, visit us online at
TANBooks.com**

**Or call us toll-free at
(800) 437-5876**